D1390917

TRAINING A TIGER

The Official Book on
How to be the Best

BY Earl Woods
WITH Pete McDaniel

796·352

FOREWORD BY Tiger Woods

Hodder & Stoughton

ISBN 0 340 70737 2

Printed and bound in Great Britain by
Mackays of Chatham PLC, Chatham, Kent

Hodder and Stoughton
A division of Hodder Headline PLC
338 Euston Road
London NW1 3BH

This work of love is dedicated to the one person most responsible for the nurturing and development of my personal values, sense of morality, and concept of self—my mother, Maude Ellen Carter Woods. And what a grand lady she was! Educated with wisdom far ahead of her time, she suffered the dehumanizing effects of prejudice without succumbing to the bitterness and hostility it engendered in others. With education a priority, she raised six children, four of whom received college degrees.

Her counseling was simple:

- "Never judge others—we already have a professional who is uniquely qualified for the job."

- "Get your education. That is something no one can EVER, EVER take away from you."

- "You have to be better than others to get an equal opportunity."

- "Share and care."

- "And finally, always be a good person."

CONTENTS

ACKNOWLEDGMENTS

I would like to take this opportunity to acknowledge Paul Fregia of Chicago, Illinois, whose idea it was to do this project. Without you, my man, it would not have been completed. Thanks for administering those "attitude adjustments" you have so subtly pulled on me during the dog days.

And to the immense group of people, too numerous to name, who provided support of all kinds to the growth and development of Tiger as a golfer and person. You all know who you are! Thanks from the bottom of my heart. Your contributions will always be appreciated and never, ever forgotten!

FOREWORD BY TIGER WOODS

So much has been written about my development as a golfer that sometimes even I have a difficult time distinguishing between fact and fiction. The one thing that I know for certain is that without the love, support, and guidance of my parents, I would not have had the opportunities I have enjoyed in life or golf. My father said something once during an interview that I think accurately sums up my relationship with him and Mom: "My son was subconciously secure, knowing that whatever parameters we established, he could always be confident that behind him was parental power and strength."

There is so much truth in that statement. My parents have been behind me from the beginning. Their teachings assist me in almost every decision I make. They are my foundation.

I am told that my love affair with golf began before I could talk or walk. Of course, I don't remember sitting in my high chair in the garage watching Pop hit balls. But what I do remember is an early fascination with the game because Pop seemed to enjoy it so much. In retrospect, golf for me was an apparent attempt to emulate the person I looked up to more than anyone: my father.

Because I started playing golf at such an early age, my father was forced to apply unique and creative teaching techniques. These techniques enabled him to teach me the fundamentals of the game while keeping it simple, fun, competitive, and challenging at all times. He says I was unusually attentive for my age. I was also very eager to learn as much as I could about the game that had so thoroughly captivated my father. I remember a daily ritual we had when I was a child: I would call Pop at work to ask if I could practice with him. He would always pause for a second or two—keeping me in suspense—but he always said yes. Then Mom would drop me off at the golf course to meet Pop for practice. In his own way he was teaching me initiative. You see, he never pushed me to play. Whether I practiced or played was always my idea. He was instrumental in helping me develop the drive to achieve, but his role—as well as my mother's—was one of support and guidance, not interference, well-meaning or otherwise.

After meeting with my father for a practice session, we would go directly to the pitching area to hit balls. The pitching area was like a driving range for me because, as you might imagine, I couldn't hit the ball very far. Well, my horizons have expanded since then.

Pop and I would finish hitting balls and head for the putting green, where we would compete for hours like two old adversaries. We'd have the greatest time playing all kinds of putting games. Since I couldn't hit it on the same level as him, I knew that I could make up for it through putting. He swears he let me win sometimes, but I believe I won some of those puttings contests fair and square. One of my favorite traditions was a trip to the nineteenth hole for a drink after practice. We would both order our usual: Mine was a Coke with cherries; Pop preferred something a bit stronger.

The best thing about those practices was that my father always kept it fun. It is amazing how much you can learn when you truly enjoy doing something. Golf for me has always been a labor of love and pleasure, although sometimes impatience got the better of me. Every time that happened, Pop would remind me how important it is to prepare for life's challenges so that I could face them confidently. He would use golf to teach me about patience, integrity, honesty, and humility. We haven't always agreed, and I was always encouraged to voice my opinion. But when he would tell me, "Son, you get out of it what you put into it," I understood exactly what he meant: that no one is going to give you anything in life unless you work hard and bust your rear end, and even then charity might not come your way. He helped establish my work ethic early, and for that I'll forever be grateful.

I hope you can find a way to give to your son or daughter what my father has given me through this wonderful game. Use it as a vehicle to teach them about life. Thanks to Mom and Pop, those teachings continue to work for me.

INTRODUCTION

My father was infatuated with baseball. He knew the names, batting averages, and pitching statistics of most players in the major leagues but was particularly proud of his heroes in the Negro Leagues. He shared that love with me, the youngest of his six children. So when word came that the Homestead Grays were bringing their barnstorming tour to Manhattan, Kansas, wild horses could not have kept me away.

I was exposed to the great American pastime at an early age. My father used to put up the huge black numbers on the scoreboard at the municipal ballpark, and I was a batboy when the black teams came to town. By the time I turned thirteen, I had earned all-state honors several times in Little League. My first year in American Legion ball, I made all-state as a catcher—the first black in Kansas to be so honored.

I had a gun for an arm and was eager to show it off. My opportunity came on that dusty summer day when the baggy-uniformed Grays put on their show against the fully bearded House of David troupe.

The catcher Roy Campanella was my idol. From his knees he could throw out the speediest base runner. You can imagine his reaction when, as a rather brash small-town boy, I sauntered up to him and bragged that with my major-league arm I could do the same. He didn't laugh me off the field, but he eyed me with more than a little skepticism. He indulged nonetheless, tossed me his glove, and allowed me to warm up the great pitcher Satchel Paige.

I told Campy to tell Satch on the last pitch to duck, because the ball's coming right through his chest. He laughed but he did as I instructed. And when Satch threw that last pitch, I really fired that sucker at his chest. The second baseman sat there and took it off his ankle. I walked over to Campy and gave him the glove. He said, "Boy, you do have a major-league arm."

My father wasn't there to see it. He had died two years before. But I know he was smiling in the great beyond, although the smile probably faded some years later when the son he had always wanted to be a pro ballplayer chose the path to higher learning instead.

So you see, baseball, not golf, was my first love; my adoration for the game that has been so much a part of my life did not come until years later. My preparation began with a desire to compete at the highest level fostered by my mother, Maude. She had a college degree but was unable to get a job in the school system and went to work as a maid for people who weren't nearly as educated as she. She saw that the road to success in the future was education and insisted that my brother, sisters, and I follow that road. She used to say, "You're going to have to be better than the other people to have an equal opportunity." Mom died when I was thirteen, and my oldest sister, Hattie, raised me. But I never forgot Mom's lessons of life, and I took them with me to Kansas State University as a scholarship baseball player.

I faced a major decision at the end of my freshman year when the Kansas City Monarchs of the Negro League offered me a contract to play for them. That night, mulling it over, I heard voices: my mother's voice saying, "Son, get your education—that's something no one can ever take away from you"; and my father saying, "Son, I want you to be a Kansas City Monarch"; then my mother again, "Get your education, son. You hear what I say?" Well, my mother won. I never regretted the decision. I continued to play at Kansas State, where I was the only black player in the entire Big Eight conference.

During those years I started my second profession: teaching. As a way of giving back to the Little League, which had been a big part of my development into an all-star catcher, I would whip together an all-star team and take them to the state tournament. Working with kids proved a very interesting and rewarding experience from which I learned patience. Helping to shape youths, watching them succeed, and nurturing them through failure is something I'll never forget. Teaching was almost second nature to me, perhaps a product of my formative years under the watchful eye of my mother and sisters. So that's what I did after graduation and a summer of semipro ball.

Later I joined the Army, where I became a teacher of young men in all sorts of subjects and endeavors. While teaching at City College of New York, my association with young cadets was close and personal. They approached my class with so much enthusiasm that many requested permission for their girlfriends to share in the experience of learning military history, tactics, and war games. I agreed. The young women joined in the discussions, and I believe, benefited from the instruction. At the end of the class, my cadets gave me a silver plaque that read, TO SIR, WITH LOVE.

The bottom line is that I love to teach, to give of myself, to share the knowledge and experiences that I have with others, because I believe I can communicate the lessons I've learned. And it is heartwarming to see the lightbulb go on with some student who understands what I'm talking about. It is a light I've seen many times with my own son. And it is one I hope you will see often with your child in teaching the game of golf.

Of course, my education continued in the service. I learned about discipline and had my father's theories of teamwork reinforced. I also saw the world and, in two tours of Vietnam as a Green Beret, stared death in the face more than once. I also met and fought side by side with a Vietnamese officer and Tiger's namesake, Lieutenant Colonel Nguyen T. Phong. I had become an information officer years earlier, and it was on one of those information assignments that I met Tiger's mother, Kultida. I had three children from an earlier marriage and was not eager to embark on a new relationship, but my heart guided me, and I was given a second chance not only at happiness but also, later on, at parenting. In retrospect, all of my experiences must have been God's doing, His way of preparing me to handle the mission of guiding this young man that was coming. Even the fact that I had three children was like Him saying, "I'll give him a trial run. Let him have some children and see how he handles it, but he's got to be able to do everything. I want him to know how difficult it is because I want the best for Tiger." Lo and behold, I did it. All my years as a teacher, sharing with and caring for others, was helping prepare me to teach Tiger. I feel blessed, but quite frankly, when Tiger was a little boy, I used to say, "Why me, Lord? What have I done to deserve this beautiful and special kid?" I never heard an answer, so I must have been doing a good enough job, because if I'd have been ticking Him off, He would have probably let me know, and I wouldn't be around writing this book for you.

I have related the story many times about my introduction to the game of golf. And I swear it is true. I was a forty-two-year-old lieutenant colonel stationed at Fort Hamilton in Brooklyn, New York. A fellow officer invited me to play with him. A southerner who grew up caddying for his father, who was a professional—a rarity among blacks in those days—this brash so-called friend actually goaded me into playing. He knew my reputation as a competitor and played on that. I had never even picked up a club, but responding to a challenge, off I went. I had no clubs, so as soon as we got out of sight of the starter, my friend gave me one of his irons and instructed me to hit down on the ball. I produced a mighty blow that barely moved the ball but reverberated to China. No doubt his cackling could be heard three fairways over. I gradually improved over the course of the round, shot 92 for seventeen holes and realized there was more to the game than just hitting down on the ball. My friend delighted in telling anyone who would listen how badly he had beaten me. Not only was I frustrated and intrigued by this new game, but I was determined to improve quicker than anyone ever had and beat my friend. It was a matter of pride.

There was only one problem: My friend was scheduled to retire in six weeks. That didn't give me much time, but I worked diligently on my game, mostly in secret. Three days before his retirement, I laid down the gauntlet. We set up the match at Fort Dix, New Jersey, and I brought along another friend as the official scorer. Not only did I beat him, which left him in stunned disbelief, but during my preparation for the match, I found that I had become addicted to the game.

It was then I decided that if I ever had another child, he or she would be exposed to the game earlier than I had been. And along came Tiger. By the time he was born, I was nearly a scratch player, so God's game plan was already in effect. I had been properly trained and was ready to go. I took over new ground in starting Tiger at an unthinkably early age and developed teaching techniques that were easily communicated to him.

The Almighty entrusted this precocious child to me. He is orchestrating this entire scenario and has a plan to utilize Tiger to make an impact on the world. I don't know what it is, but I sincerely believe it will be spiritual and humanitarian and will transcend the game of golf.

The average parents will go through the full gamut of ups and downs and trials and tribulations when raising normal kids. The key is developing closer ties with your children, teaching them to perform and function effectively. Golf is an excellent vehicle for reaching those objectives. And if you as parents can teach your children to love and respect the game of golf, they will inevitably learn all these associated lessons about life. This book is my way of giving back to a game that has given me so much. I believe that if you take advantage of what I have learned and apply these lessons to your child, you may not raise a champion golfer, but you will raise a better person, one who can face life's challenges confidently. And that is about as good as it gets for us parents. The rest is up to them.

—EARL WOODS
January 1997

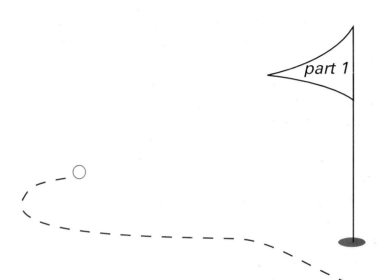

part 1

Preparations

DEVELOP A RELATIONSHIP

1

Trust, Respect, Communication, Relationship, Truth, Terminology

Developing a relationship with your child based on love and respect is a prerequisite for nurturing his or her natural curiosity. A good environment promotes trust and paves the way for communication, the foundation for learning. It all begins with the parent's desire to make the child's life better, to enhance his or her probability of success in life. What the parent has to do is say, "I want my child to have it better than I. I want my child to have more opportunities and more support. I want my child to be better prepared to handle life than I was. I want my child to be more success-ful. I want my child to be rewarded for effort." The rela-tionship between parent and child must be built on mutual respect. In order for that to happen, the parent must under-

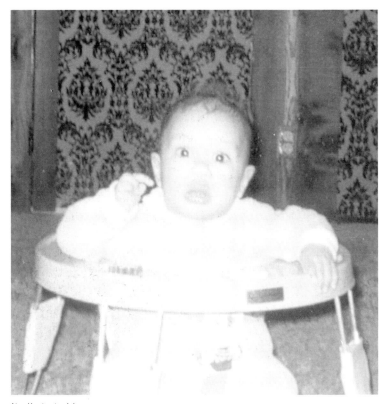

It all started here.

stand that love is given and respect earned. The parent must start at as early an age as possible to earn that respect. Convey to the child that you care, that you are there like an oak in support. Counsel only when needed. Laugh and cry with your child. And, above all, be consistent. A child can be thrown off by waffling. While earning your child's respect, you must reciprocate. It is part of the learning process. When it clicks, you will discover that your child is receptive to things that you thought he or she might not be. Things work. Life is good.

Be reassuring. You can never say to a child too often that I love you. A parent has to make the commitment right off the bat to be selfless, responsible, and put the child first.

When Tiger came home from the hospital at five days old, I did two things. I wanted jazz music to be the first music he heard. So I cranked up the stereo, and when he heard it, he smiled. I established my personal imprint on his mind, at least about musical preference. Of course, years later, he succumbed to the rap craze, the thump,

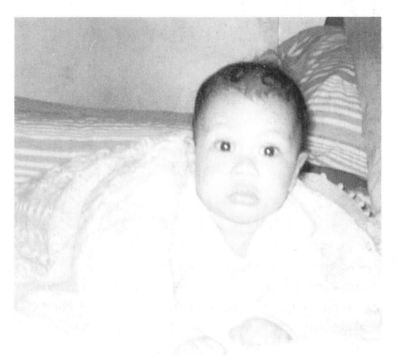

A wide-eyed Tiger ready to receive his first club.

thump of which almost drove his mother and me crazy. He has since returned to his roots, and we have shared many evenings enjoying jazz.

An enjoyable day at the park with Mom and Toba

I also talked to him as he lay in his crib while stroking his left cheek with my index finger. I would say, "Daddy loves you. I am here for you. You're my little man. Daddy is so proud of you. I want you to be happy"—the same little terms of endearment that most parents use. When he was asleep, I would go to his crib and touch his cheek, and he would smile. He knew it was me. He will know it for the rest of his life.

When Tiger got older, I established a kind of an open-door policy between us that whenever he wanted to talk to me, everything else—TV, stereo, the works—went off. We would go into another room and talk—not about what I wanted to talk about but what he wanted to talk about. Whatever subject came up, we would hash it out until he brought up another one. And when I didn't have the answers for my little inquisitor, I would be honest and admit that I didn't know. I established credibility and respect. I would also promise to try and find the answer, and more often than not I would.

A parent should make time to spend with the child. It is not always easy in this age of two-job households, but I believe time is a product of one's desires and priorities. If your priority is your child, you will find time. And it will be quality time because the child knows the difference between thoughtful answers and offhanded remarks. You must always be aware that you are conveying to your child that you care. Offer direction and guidance, too, in small doses initially and always fairly and compassionately.

This golfing journey of learning must be a cooperative endeavor, upheld equally by husband and wife. Both must have the same desires and aspirations for their child. It is a team effort. One cannot be contradictory or contrary to the aims of the other. Early on we sat down and decided that Tiger would be the first priority in our relationship from that point on, that Tida would stay home and raise Tiger and that since I had recently retired from the military service, I would enter the workplace and earn a living. We decided always to be truthful and consistent, thereby establishing parameters for Tiger's conduct and performance.

In the earliest stages of a child's development, uncondi-
tional love is of vital importance. From this total acceptance,
this constant reminder that "I love you, I'll always be here
for you," Tiger blossomed like a beautiful spring flower.

Some of you might encounter a rebellious attitude in
your child. Rebellion is a way of asserting independence.
By respecting and acknowledging this, you can redirect
these outbursts into positive experiences without stripping
your child of his or her pride. Stand firm and be the parent.
Knowing the "limits" will give your child a sense of secu-
rity even as he or she chafes at theses strictures. A child
with a strong personality is forever testing and probing to
see just how far negative behavior will take him. Gently but
firmly remind him that these acts will result in a negative
response from you but that love is always there to protect
him.

One of Tida's major contributions was to establish that
school took priority over golf and any other activity. She
insisted that Tiger complete his homework before playing
with his friends, going to practice with me, or playing in a
tournament. Much like my mother, Tida believed that edu-
cating the mind was the avenue to success. And she would
tell Tiger that while there were no guarantees he would be
successful in golf, with an educated mind he could be successful in business and, more importantly, in life. "You
must always have something to fall back on," she would
say. "You can get injured; you may have an illness; but with
an education you can always contribute to society."

Tiger was Tida's only child, and she would ask me, "How
do I act? How do I treat my child?" I told her, "Follow your

At five months, athletic balance is demonstrated.

instincts and be who you are. If you make mistakes, they will be honest mistakes. And I'll always be there to help." In my opinion, and I'm sure Tiger's, too, she has made very few.

Her teaching methods weren't always orthodox, but they were effective. When Tiger was just a toddler, she wrote the addition and multiplication tables out for him on 3-by-5-inch cards, and he would practice them over and over every day. He started with addition and later advanced to multiplication as he got older. His reward was an afternoon on the practice range with me. Tida established irrevocably that education had a priority over golf.

You might ask, "Is all of this nurturing necessary?" I believe it is if your aim is developing a strong and lasting relationship with your child, one based on trust and communication. You as a parent have a lot of learning to do yourself, not only about your child but about yourself. I have found that in my life when I gave to and shared with others, I almost always ended up helping myself. I got a better understanding of who I was, and my life improved as a result.

Christmas celebration with his first golf club, five days before his first birthday

Things don't always go smoothly. You must allow room for disagreement. In fact, I always encouraged Tiger to question what I was saying and, if he found me in error, to let me know so I could learn, too. In this way parents can learn from their children as well. Not many children are afforded that opportunity because most parents don't want to make themselves vulnerable like that. You could never be laid more bare than I was with Tiger during some of our first golf outings. He was eighteen months old, couldn't count to five, but he intuitively knew a par–5 from a par–4 and a par–3. He would keep score of not only his strokes but mine, too. He'd say, "Daddy, you got a double bogey." Now, that was six strokes and he couldn't count to five. It was amazing. He was watching how many strokes it took to get to the green and how many putts you took. Evidently, he added all this up in his head and came out with a phrase or number. And it wasn't six or seven, it was double bogey or triple bogey. So you see, I couldn't "massage" my golf scores, not around Tiger.

One of the toughest things I had to teach Tiger was the

Yeah, I made it!

need for a preshot routine or procedure. In the military we called it standard operating procedure (SOP). Whenever you could quantify something or make it routine, you'd put an SOP out on it. Then you didn't have to reinvent the wheel each time. It became automatic and rote and thus more effective. SOP is based on problem and solution. The problem was getting Tiger to understand that in golf every shot starts behind the ball. Only from that position can one visualize the shot and plan proper execution. The solution was to develop a routine procedure so that Tiger could perform under pressure as effectively as he did in the absence of it. So the SOP approach was used to establish a preshot routine. He didn't like the idea that every shot should start from behind the ball, so we had a big discussion about it. Finally I asked him, "Doesn't every shot start with a target?" He answered in the affirmative. I said, "What better way to determine your target than to stand behind your ball and look at it?"

"Daddy, you know that's right," said my three-year-old. "That's a good idea." So we implemented the preshot routine.

Then I showed him how he should mentally go over all the necessary conditions that would affect his shot. I don't think a normal three-year-old could have comprehended what I was trying to teach him, but Tiger was not a normal child of three. We did it with questions and answers. I asked him, "What do you have to know before you can hit the ball?"

He responded, "How far I have to hit it, my distance."

I asked, "What else?"

"What about the wawa?" he answered.

I said, "Yes, the wawa is one."

He said, "How about the sand twap?"

"Yes," I responded, "the sand twap, but there's some other stuff, too."

He said, "If my ball's in a divot."

"That's called your lie. That's another one, but what about"—and I made a blowing noise with my mouth."

"Oh, the wind, Daddy, the wind," he said, his eyes widening as if he'd made a great discovery. We just made a big, wonderful game of it, and pretty soon we had covered all the elements he had to go through before he selected a club leading to the completion of his preshot routine. He also developed a comparable putting routine.

Eventually, Tiger accepted the need for a preestablished routine, and today he uses the same one I taught him those many years ago. I also have one for myself—different, but performing the same function. We learned together. There was a metamorphosis, and all of a sudden we became friends, not just parent and child. And I think you'll agree there's nothing more important in the world today than having a friend, especially when that friend is your own child.

WHEN TO START

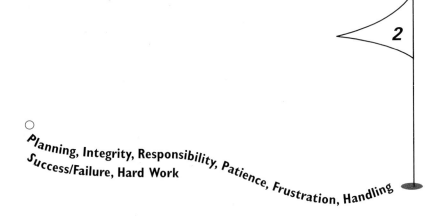

2

Planning, Integrity, Responsibility, Patience, Frustration, Handling Success/Failure, Hard Work

In order to get an athlete to perform a sport instinctively, you must start the learning process when the child is young enough so that the performance of the game is totally ingrained and flows from the subconscious. For example, when do parents give their sons a baseball glove and ball? Many times it is when they're in the crib, and the child grows up instinctively knowing how to throw a baseball and how to catch it. My objective was to bring the same approach to golf. I wanted Tiger to grow up feeling as natural swinging a club as a baseball child feels throwing a baseball.

There is no single, standard guideline about when to start your child. It depends on many factors, not the least of which is the gut feeling of the parent about when the child is ready—not when the parent is ready. After all, who knows a child better than a parent? A lot of it depends on the maturity of the child, how receptive the child is to new adventures. If there is more than one child in the family, it becomes easier because you can teach them at the same time. Don't be surprised if the younger sibling learns more quickly; the older one is like a minitutor teaching what has already been learned from you or other sources. Children

Practice also includes bunker play, even at two years, eight months.

learn by observation and imitation. Tiger would sit in his high chair in the garage and watch me hit balls into the net. Before I knew it, he was imitating my golf swing.

15

Mom tees it up for Tiger on Navy golf course driving range (age two years, seven months).

Three years

Allow the child's natural curiosity to exert itself and take hold. There might be a club just sitting around the household; the child picks it up and starts playing with it, trying to figure out what to do with it. Perhaps the child will come to you and ask what this thing is used for. You seize the opportunity, and there is your child's entry into the game.

Arbitrary imposition of the game is guaranteed to bring about negative results. It should be a willing, cooperative, exciting time: You're not only teaching your child about golf but also about our societal values, customs, and traditions. Let's face it: Your child is learning about life. The byproducts of golf are integrity, responsibility, and patience. The

17

game builds character, and it can start with a plastic ball and club placed in your child's crib. Babies learn rapidly. They will associate the club with the ball and make hitting the ball a game. They are learning the framework and basics of a game without any outside influence.

Of course, the ideal situation would be for your child to come to you and say, "I saw golf on television and I'd love to learn to play it." That would be ideal, opening up a dialogue about the game. But it isn't going to happen very often. So parents interested in introducing the game to their children must be creative yet practical.

For parents who are golfers, it is beneficial to practice in front of your children *if* you have a good golf swing—you do not want to teach bad habits that are hard to break. But you do want to show them your enthusiasm, your love for the game, how much fun it is to hit the ball. They pick up on enthusiasm right away and want to be a part of it. "Please, can I hit one?" they implore. You agree but never let them hit too many. Always keep them wanting more.

You may be concerned about how to keep your child's attention. The answer is by making golf interesting and fun. Through the use of guile and imagination, you create an attractive and stimulating forum for the game. That's the sheer joy and challenge of good parenting. You'll love it!

I was lucky. Tiger took to the game immediately. Much like me, he had an instant infatuation with it. And I always kept him wanting more. He was two years old when he memorized my telephone number at work, and he would call me at the office in the afternoon and ask, "Daddy, can I practice with you today?"

After a pause where I had him worrying that I would say no, I'd say, "All right."

He would answer,"OK, Daddy, I'll see you at the golf course. I'll have Mommy bring me over." He always felt energized when he came to the course because he felt he'd pulled something over on me. He had earned the right because Mom had performed her daily ritual of helping him with his addition, subtraction, multiplication, and so on, before he was permitted to call me. I never let him get tired and kept it challenging, competitive, and fun.

One of the biggest hurdles to clear when teaching your child to play golf is frustration. Most children get turned off when they can't master something quickly. In golf, as in life, there is no instant gratification. You must show them that you haven't mastered it either—no one ever does—but you're still playing and enjoying it. In fact, you're out there working very hard to improve. This provides a perfect opportunity to illustrate one of life's lessons: You aren't necessarily successful every time you attempt new endeavors, but if you continue to strive to improve, you will at least know you gave it your all. Never mention the word *failure*. Always accentuate the positive. "I like the way you swing the club. It won't be long before you are hitting it a ton!" Positive reinforcement and emphasis on the need to practice are a winning combination. When people would ask Tiger how he got so good, he would smile and say, "Practice, practice, practice, oooh!" Where this "oooh" came from I don't know, but that's what he would say.

Sometimes no matter how good your intentions, your child might show no interest in golf. Don't despair. This indifference, which is more common than you might think, is best countered if you become more involved in the sport that does interest your child. Find a way to teach the things you want to in life through that sport. Always remain supportive. Never close the door to golf; keep the child's options open, and occasionally mention how much fun you have playing

Three years, eight months

your game. Invite the child along to practice with you, but do not insist. Openly discuss the nuances of your game, and tie them in with your child favorite sport. Say, "I know you have a ball shooting hoops because it's fun. When I was young, I used to shoot hoops all the time, too, but I was not very good at it. Sometimes I would only make one out of ten shots, and

Five years: The swing gets better with age.

sometimes now I only make one out of five putts, but when I make that one, it feels as good as when you make a 20-foot jump shot." Make comparisons the child can relate to. Meanwhile, you're planting seeds: Let them grow and nurture them. Over time, if nothing else, your child will have a greater appreciation and understanding of your game, and you will have a greater appreciation and understanding of your child's sport. It may take years for your child to become interested in golf. You cannot force it. All you can do is leave the door open. I walked through it when I was forty-two, so there is hope for everyone.

21

How to Work Together

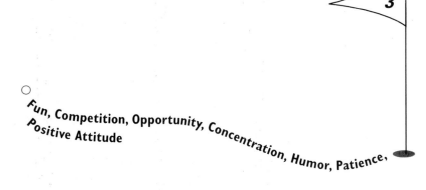

3

Fun, Competition, Opportunity, Concentration, Humor, Patience, Positive Attitude

The optimal situation would be for your child to come to you as Tiger would come to me and say, "Daddy, can I practice with you today?" But that isn't necessarily going to occur in every household, so you must take care to ensure that the child does not receive the signal that he or she is being forced into something. Make your child believe that participating in golf is fun, and you want to share that.

The best way I have found to work with children is to offer a challenge. Children respond readily to challenges. "Let's see how good you are." You must be a little roguish, intentionally losing a game every now and then, because— let's face it—your skill level will probably be greater than theirs in the beginning. But I assure you, it is inevitable that they will eventually be better than you, just as Tiger quickly became better than I.

There are two times that are the "first" time that Tiger beat me. On one occasion, we were playing a par–3 course called Heartwell in Long Beach. Tiger was eight years old, and I hate to say it, but he did beat me, although I wasn't really trying my best, so I don't acknowledge it as a true defeat. It is still disputed today, but I must admit that when he said, "Daddy, I beat you," they were the sweetest words I'd ever heard. In my record book Tiger first really beat me when he was eleven. I was trying my best, but he honestly whipped me. I haven't come close to beating him since, and I never will. So parents be warned, you are creating a monster! But it is a beautiful monster, this skilled young student. And you will be so proud and happy to witness the development of your child not only as a golfer but as a person. The two go hand in hand.

Children respond best when their interest is piqued. The surest way to keep their attention is to make golf fun. Parents should consistently present a positive and patient attitude. There are several ways to accomplish this, but I have found the best way is through competitive games. A little oneupmanship can go a long way toward attracting and sustaining your child's interest. Later in the book I will list in detail a number of games and competitions that you can use as teaching aids. They are also useful in teaching your child the etiquette of golf—the rules and acceptable behavior. For example, "Never run on the green, always fix your divots, and repair your ball marks." They will also help in developing a golfing vocabulary. Yes, golf has its own vocabulary, both technical and nontechnical. In teaching a child the game, you have to communicate. You must deliver a message, and the receipt of that message must be acknowledged.

The challenge lies in making sure that the message has been understood so that real learning can take place.

Most parents will be further advanced in their technical knowledge than their child. Explanations must be simple and direct. In the case of a younger child, the parent must be prepared to demonstrate, verbalize, and then demonstrate again and again and again until he child understands and gives the proper feedback.

Setup, weight distribution, and balance are part of the golfing vocabulary. I taught Tiger what each one meant through demonstration. I started with the ready position to hit the ball: feet spread comfortably apart, knees flexed, waist and hips parallel to the feet. I explained it step by step, and then I explained it again. He could not grasp the meaning of *parallel*. As a one-year-old, he had a backswing that would go past parallel so that the club was pointing toward the ground. He kept that swing until one day, a couple of years later, we were invited to Santa Ana Country Club to put on an exhibition. The head pro took a Polaroid picture of Tiger's swing, and it showed Tiger's club pointing to the ground. I used the photo to illustrate to Tiger what I meant by *parallel*. "See where your club is right here?" I said to him, pointing to the downward club in his backswing. "That is too far in your backswing. This is where it should be, parallel to the ground." I ran my finger laterally along his shoulder line and along the ground. "This is parallel, when two lines are like this."

Parallel position

"Oh," he said. Since that day he has never taken the club past parallel.

Children learn quickly, especially when it comes to scoring terminology. A par is the number of shots a first-rate golfer would make going from the tee to the hole. It varies with the length of the hole: usually par–5, par–4, and par–3. Each par is predicated upon having two putts to get the ball into the hole. A par–4 is long enough that the normal golfer—John Daly notwithstanding—cannot reach the green with a single shot. It is designed to be reached in two shots and then two

25

putts—hence par–4. A bogey is when par is exceeded by one stroke, and a double bogey is when par is exceeded by two strokes, and so on.

When Tiger first started playing, I would assign par for him. He knew what that par was, and some of our biggest arguments came when I changed his par. For example, his par on a 390-yard hole was 7, which meant he was given five shots to reach the green and two putts to make par. As he got older and began to hit the ball farther, he could reach the green with fewer strokes. So I would reduce his par. "No, no," he would say. Par was no longer good enough. He wanted to make birdie. It was the beginning of a competitive desire that knows no comfort zone. By that I mean when Tiger is five under par, he wants to be six under par. When he's six under par, he wants to be seven. He does not say, "Wow, I'm five under. I'm not supposed to be shooting like this." The truth is Tiger has been shooting like that since he was two years old. He's been shooting five, six, seven under par with those assigned pars. We argued because he always wanted to be under par. We have laughed about it many times since. He never realized that I was giving him strokes. What started with fun competitive games developed into a shared learning experience and closeness from which we both continue to benefit. I'm sure you and your child will also.

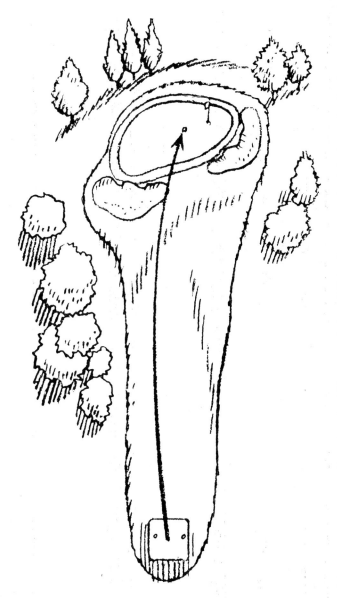

Illustration of a typical par–3 . . .

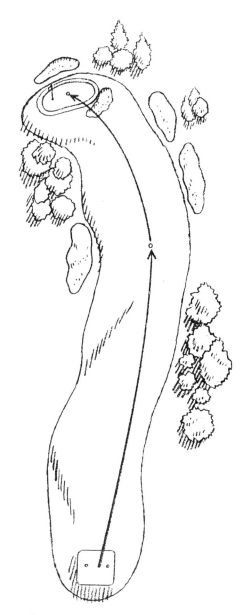

par–4 . . .

and par–5.

EQUIPMENT

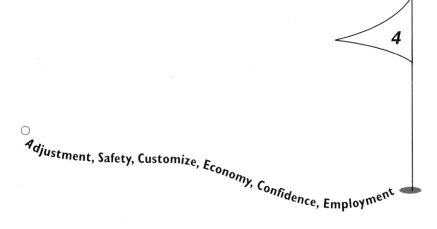

4

Adjustment, Safety, Customize, Economy, Confidence, Employment

To play the game, some equipment is necessary—not a lot in the earliest stages of development, but it should be appropriate for the age and size of your child. The three most critical factors are the overall weight, length, and thickness of the grip of a club. You wouldn't think of giving your nine-year-old a 36-inch baseball bat, but you might not think anything about giving him a full-length, adult-size golf club. Care must be taken to ensure that clubs fit properly not only initially, but throughout the developmental growth period of your child. An additional element to consider is the loft of the club. It should be a 7-, 8- or 9-iron. This facilitates your child's ability to hit the ball into the air. It's no fun dribbling every shot along the ground. But just watch your child's eyes light up when the ball goes into the air. The game is on. Your child is hooked.

There is no need to obtain a large number of clubs. One iron and a putter are enough to begin with—consistent, however, with proper size and weight. Manufacturers have recently begun to market plastic clubs and balls and graphite shafted clubs (lightweight and functional). These are reasonably priced and available in sporting-goods stores and golf pro shops.

Custom repair facilities will gladly construct a club for your child at a reasonable price. That is how I initially equipped Tiger. He has used the Custom Golf House in Orange, California, since taking up the game. Bill Orr, the proprietor and owner, has earned Tiger's respect so much that he will not permit any other professional to adjust his clubs. You can develop a similar relationship with one of your local club-repair experts and benefit from their expertise and advice for years to come. I would suggest parents not take on this task of cutting down and sizing clubs because it could easily become counterproductive. You might cut the club too short; then you've ruined a club. It requires special tape to create a grip for a club. Then you must know the correct size of grip in order to fit the hands of your child. All this trouble can be avoided if you leave the work up to the experts. And quite frankly, the expense is not prohibitive. Prices may vary, depending upon section of the country, but you can expect to pay somewhere between $15 and $20 for the construction of one golf club.

Tiger's first club was a 7-iron that had the back of the face machined off to make it lighter. The grip was a different problem because he started at such an early age. The iron had to be shortened so much that no grip would fit because the shaft was too small in diameter. The solution was to build up the shaft with regular household tape so that the grip would fit. Ironically, the grip fit, but it was too big for his hands, so Bill and I had to make more adjustments until we got it right. And do you know who the harshest, most demanding critic was? Tiger. He wanted it to fit right. His insistence on correct fitting caused me to promise myself that I would always see to it that Tiger's equipment was the right size for him throughout his growing years.

The putter is a slightly different story. By the very nature of its design, it can be reduced in size and be perfectly functional for a child. I recommend a heel-and-toe weighted putter for balance and ease of striking the ball. Length is critical in helping your child to avoid bad habits. If you have seen the noted Japanese professional Isao Aoki with the toe of his putter pointing in the air, you know what I mean. This habit can undoubtedly be traced to his having had a putter at a very early age that was too long for him.

Tiger received his first real metal putter when he was seven months old. He would walk around the house in his circular walker dragging this little putter with him. He never broke anything, and it was his favorite toy. At ten months, he would use this same club to hit his first golf ball in our garage. So there you have it: a 7-iron, which was the correct loft, and a putter. That's all he used for the first year or so of his development.

Depending upon the age, your child may need more clubs. If so, you should obtain a starter set with bag, which is easily obtainable through certain retail outlets. By getting the bag, the child has a way of transporting the clubs and also develops the habit of carrying them. This is a good habit because all junior tournaments require contestants to carry their own bag and clubs. There are no caddies or carts. Tiger's first golf bag was designed and hand-sewn by his mother. Many of you might recall seeing Tiger at age two on the *Mike Douglas Show,* where he had a putting and driving contest with Bob Hope. The bag that he carried on the stage that night was a culmination of love and creativity on the part of his mother.

Have you noticed that we have your child playing a game with only a club and no ball? That was not an oversight—at this stage the ball is the least important piece of equipment. You can make up and use any ball that you want. For safety's sake, I would strongly suggest, at least initially, the use of a plastic or soft rubber ball. Even a tennis ball. Your options are endless. Wiffle-type golf balls, available in sporting-goods stores, are particularly effective and child friendly.

After reaching a degree of proficiency, your child will undoubtedly want a full set of clubs. Again, size, weight, and length are of paramount importance. I recommend that the set be limited to a putter, sand wedge, pitching wedge, and 5-iron through 9-iron. Let's face it: The average child doesn't possess the swing speed and strength necessary to hit a long iron (2-iron through 4-iron). So you're wasting your money if you include those in the set.

I know your children are no different from mine, and they want to hit the ball as far as they can. This requires a wood. I suggest no more than two, possibly a 5- or 7-wood—and for older children, in their teens, a 3-wood. The loft on the 5- and 7-woods increases the child's ability to hit the ball into the air. This breeds confidence and certainly increases enjoyment. After all, the purpose is to hit the ball and have fun while you're doing it.

part 2

Learning the Golf Swing

FUNDAMENTALS AND MECHANICS

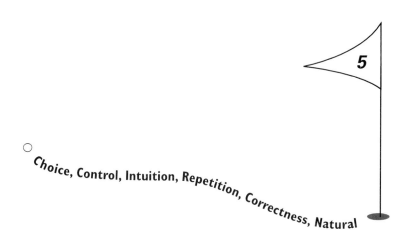

Choice, Control, Intuition, Repetition, Correctness, Natural

Golf is no different from any other game: In order to play it properly, you must master the fundamentals and mechanics. Sure, there are players who, through sheer adaptation and repetition, have managed to spin unorthodox swings into successful careers (Miller Barber and Lee Trevino come to mind), but you can bet those players were fundamentally sound in their approach to the game. They understood the importance of having a sound grip, a proper setup, a smooth tempo, and good balance.

Grip

Golf starts with the grip. Everything is transmitted through the hands to the ball, so the grip must be correct.

The baseball grip has all ten fingers on the club.

The interlock grip has the pinkie (little) finger of the right hand and the forefinger of the left interlocked.

There are three basic grips: baseball, interlock, and the Vardon or overlap. At first, allow your child to select whichever grip is most comfortable. Then, as the game becomes fun and the child becomes relatively proficient, introduce the other grips. The child will decide which one to adopt. Leave the decision entirely up to the child. Don't push it. Tiger used the baseball grip until he was six years old. He was introduced to the other two grips when he was three, but he didn't switch until he was seven, and then he used the interlock. Why the interlock? Because his hands were so small and he felt stronger with his hands locked together. Jack Nicklaus experienced a similar problem and

The Vardon grip has the right pinkie inserted into the slot between the left index finger and middle finger.

solution with small hands. After Tiger found the grip that was most comfortable and enabled him to hit the ball consistently, he never changed.

The key element in controlling the club is your hands. They are the body's point of connection to the club, and they control the direction and flight pattern of the ball. The hands must be aligned not only with each other but with the club face for direction control. The earlier you teach this, the better.

It is an easy principle to teach. I started with Tiger when he was so young that he could not talk back to me, so I had to use illustrations. I told him to clap his hands, and he extended his hands and clapped. Then I instructed him to stop and hold his palms together. Then I showed him how his hands would flex and bend as a unit. I said, "Your hands must be like this in order to hit the ball straight." Then I took the club and inserted it into his hands, aligned the club face in his hands and said, "This is the way it's supposed to look." Then I said, "OK, remember how we bent our hands?" He nodded. I said, "Now do the same thing with the club." And he got it right the first time.

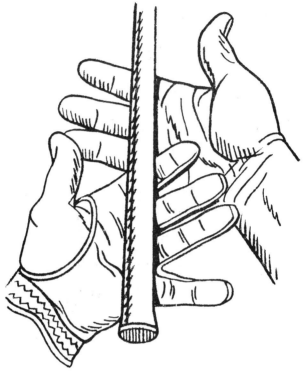

It is important to establish and maintain the grip with the
pinkie of the left hand throughout the swing.

Children as young as ten months old have an intuitive
sense of the inner self. They know when things are in balance and when things are lined up properly. It just feels
right to them. From that day on, I have never had a problem with Tiger aligning his hands with each other and
with the club face. This method will work for children of
all ages.

Here's another method you can try. Have the child stand
with his arms at his or her side. Place the club in the left

Although the club is held in all ten fingers, specific pressure points are as shown above.

hand and align the club face 90 degrees to the direction he is standing. This is the target line. In this position the left hand will naturally grip the club and be in line with the club face. The only thing remaining is to get the right hand on the club and to align it with the left. Have the child bring the club to the center of his body, and simply say, "Put your right hand on there." You might find that your child does it correctly the first time, too.

Most children will prefer the baseball grip. That's the

41

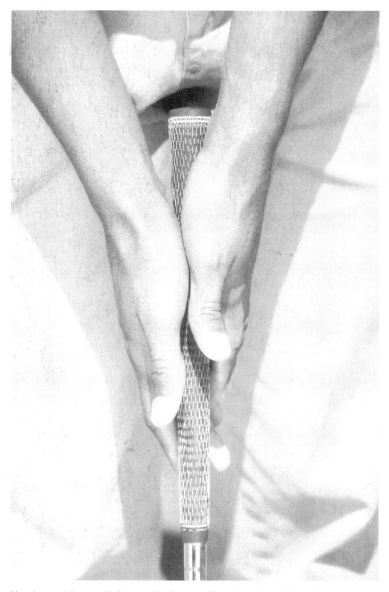

Hands must be parallel to each other to allow them to work together.

Place the butt end of the grip diagonally across the pad and junction of the left thumb and index finger.

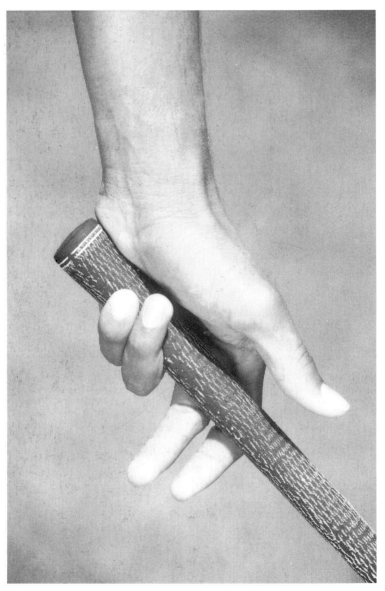

Place the last two fingers of the left hand on the grip.

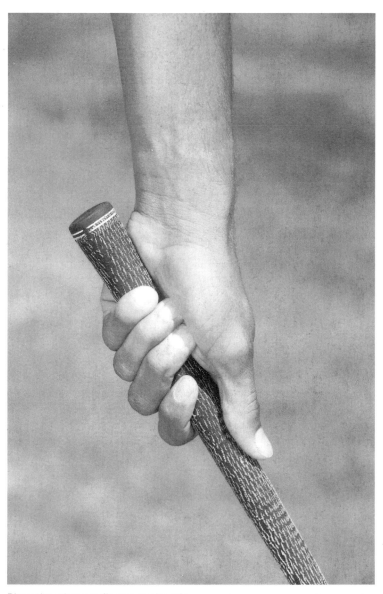

Place the other two fingers on the grip.

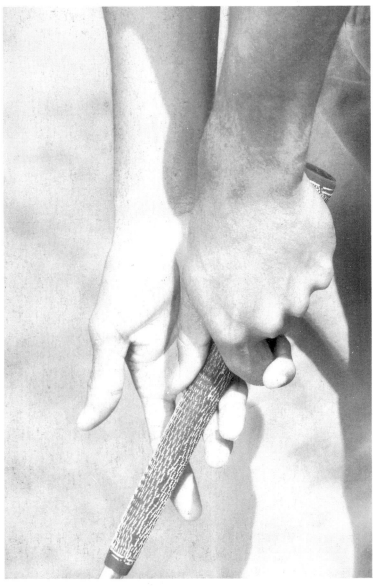

Place right hand on the grip by putting the two middle fingers on the club.

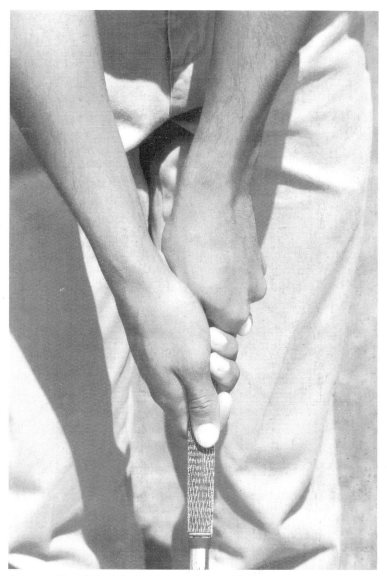

Complete the grip by bringing the remainder of right hand up and over.
Adjust until comfortable.

Side view of the completed interlock grip

way nature has built in the instincts to grasp a stick, and to them the golf club is nothing more than a metal stick with a grip on it. So don't be surprised if that is the original grip your child uses. As a parent you have to be very patient and repeat the process several times to make sure your child can do it properly without guidance. Remember the two key points are that the hands must be aligned together, and they, in turn, must be aligned with the club face. When they aren't, adjust them. While you're teaching through repetition, you're also developing a feel for correctness on the part of the child. It will become as normal and natural to your child as walking.

Setup

Just as important as teaching the proper grip is instilling in your child as early as possible the need for a sound setup, with the knees, waist, and shoulders parallel to the target line. I have talked to many professional teachers who agree that all swing faults can be traced back to the setup. It's very similar to aiming a rifle. No matter how expensive the gun, if it is not aimed properly, it will not hit the target.

A mirror is helpful in teaching the proper setup because it gives immediate visual feedback. Instruct your child to spread the feet comfortably apart; flex the knees a little; bend forward from the waist ever so slightly; relax the arms and allow them to swing freely, hanging. Then say, "Sit down just a little bit." Insert the club into the hands and say, "That's your setup."

It is important to teach the importance of balance and

This is the setup: athletic, ready for action.

placing the weight on the inside of each foot. While the child is in the setup position, slightly push on the shoulder and watch the child recoil. The child will naturally place the weight on the inside of each foot to prevent being pushed over. Point this out so that the child feels that weight. To confirm this, you can also push on the other shoulder.

Now you have a setup: weight on the inside of both feet, which are pointed outward slightly. The knees are slightly flexed; feet, hips, and shoulders parallel to one another in alignment. The weight is naturally distributed on the ball of each foot; the upper body is bent slightly forward at the waist. The arms are hanging straight to accommodate the club, and the head is set in a way that allows a natural view of the ball.

51

Here's a drill to use to ensure alignment, balance, and posture. From the setup position, have the child stand straight up with feet apart. Then bend over again, allowing the arms to hang and the knees to flex a little. Doing this over and over will contribute to the proper posture. Some people with lazy posture allow the back to hump and the

Stand straight up, then move into the setup position to ensure proper body alignment, balance, and posture.

head to drop. This is not a natural position when you're standing straight up, so if this occurs in the setup position, revert back to the standing position and correct this deficiency. The back should be reasonably straight and the head slightly raised. Notice that this is natural. There's nothing contrived about this move. If you teach these fundamentals—balance and alignment—to your child at an early age, the benefits will last a lifetime.

Tempo

Tempo is critical in all aspects of golf—from putting through chipping and pitching—and especially in the full golf swing. What is tempo? It is the total expired time necessary to execute a shot. Some people swing fast, some swing slowly. If the fast swinger tried to swing unnaturally slow, his tempo would be disrupted. If the slow swinger tried to swing fast, it would be hurried and inefficient. Every golfer must find his or her own natural swinging style and strive to maintain it throughout the swing. Under pressure a golfer will invariably revert to his or her natural tempo. In the putting stroke parents should emphasize a smooth takeaway from the ball with an unhurried transition to the forward stroke and an accelerating movement into the ball. The same applies for chipping and pitching and, with even greater force, to the full swing, with its greater length and the need to generate club-head speed. All efforts should be directed toward keeping the swing natural and smooth.

Balance

Balance is everything. The body naturally seeks its balance. It is an innate instinct. To test your child's balance, start in the standing position. Push slightly on each shoulder. That sets the weight on the inside of the feet. Push from the back, setting the weight on the balls of the feet. Repeat

Push on the right shoulder to set the weight inside both feet.

the same process in the setup position. Remind the child that he or she is now in balance. If, when you push slightly on the back, the child falls forward, it indicates that the weight is on the toes. Point this out and have the child shift his or her weight a little farther back toward the balls of the feet until the difference is apparent and balance is achieved. A final test is when there are no resulting movements when

54

you push on the shoulders and the back. Now you have an athletic setup ready to execute a dynamic golf swing.

Push against the back to set your weight properly between the ball and heel of each foot.

Tiger is a natural athlete, so his body is always in balance. But he sometimes allows his left shoulder to drop back when he goes into the setup. To cure this, I would have him go into the setup position, close his eyes, stand straight up, go back into the setup position, and then open his eyes. Invariably the natural balance would take effect, and his shoulder would be square, aligned with the rest of his body. And I would point this out to him. So when you're watching Tiger in a tournament, if he stands up after addressing the ball and goes back into the setup, you now know where it came from.

55

THE FIRST PHASE: PUTTING

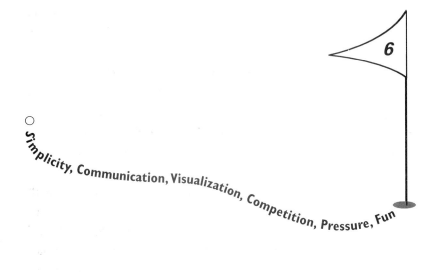

Simplicity, Communication, Visualization, Competition, Pressure, Fun

I firmly believe that in order to teach the full golf swing, you must start with the simplest golf swing, the putt, and then move on to chipping and pitching. That progression of instruction is the easiest way to teach a child how to play the game because it does not require major ball-striking ability. Golf should be taught from the green back to the tee.

◁ Putting

◁ Chipping

◁ Pitching

◁ Full Swing

It is very difficult to communicate how to putt when the child is too young to talk. Demonstration by example is the solution. A child's mind is an open book waiting to have the pages filled. I taught Tiger to putt as a toddler by using his mind to visualize the picture of the target at which he was shooting.

The nice thing about a putter is that even when you cut it down, it remains functional for children—it does not become cumbersome because of too much weight in the head. The key factors in putting are to size the putter to the height of the child and the grip to fit the hands. Once these adjustments have been made, it's time to teach the simplest of swings.

Have your child use an underhand toss of the ball with the dominant hand to a hole no more than 10 feet away. This will develop a feel for distance using an easy, natural motion that is already mastered by the child. These tosses should be in a series of three or four. Add variety by having your child make some of the tosses with eyes closed. This gives the child confidence that he or she can throw an object to a target without looking, which is a critical step in learning how to putt. Only after proficiency has been achieved do you move to the next phase. The child should be able to toss the ball consistently within one foot of the hole, including the roll. Parents can also participate and create a competitive, enjoyable game.

Teach the child how to hold the putter. Parents should not demand a complicated grip but should defer to what the child does naturally. When Tiger was starting, he used the baseball grip. Golf is a game of different styles, most of which are equally acceptable. Quite a few of the top professionals

The putting grip above has both thumbs on the top of the grip and the left forefinger across the last three fingers of the right hand.

Side view from up-target

Side view from down-target

Rear view of setup

and amateurs are using the so-called cross-handed grip, in which the dominant hand is on top. You should teach some system of setup that will facilitate alignment of the body with the hole or target, thus ensuring a putt in the proper direction. Once these two fundamentals have been taught and understood, it is time to integrate the next step: the act of putting the ball to the hole.

The initial distance should be no more than one or two feet. This will enable the child to have a higher rate of success and sustain interest. Place the ball on the green. Have the child set up to the ball, look at the hole, then at the ball, then at the hole, then at the ball again. Then ask, "Do you see the picture of the hole?" If the answer is yes, tell the child to stroke the ball to the picture without looking. (If the answer

Proficiency is achieved with the use of the putt-to-the-picture procedure.

is no, repeat the process until a picture is recorded in the child's mind.) Some children may need two looks to get a clear picture, others may need three or four. Notice the tie-in with the previous drill of tossing the ball to the hole with the eyes closed. Projecting the ball toward a visual image must be learned through repetition.

As proficiency increases, extend the distance from the hole. Using three balls, set one three feet away, another six feet, and the last ten feet. Preface each putt with the phrase, "Putt to the picture."

All putts are not on level ground, nor do they appear straight. Alignment must take into consideration slope of the green, speed of the green, and other conditions. The information regarding these conditions should be conveyed verbally. "This putt is uphill. The green is fast. The green is slow. The green is wet." This permits the child to naturally and automatically gauge the force necessary, given those conditions, to putt the ball to the picture.

All putts are straight—it's the ground that's crooked. How do you putt breaking putts: balls that move from right to left or left to right? The answer is in the setup. By looking at the hole, you make a determination that the ball will move (break) a certain number of inches to the left or right. Then set up accordingly, aiming at a corresponding distance to that side of the hole. This permits the golfer to focus on distance rather than direction because distance control is more important than direction control. By putting to the picture and allowing the human computer to function, the golfer is free to concentrate only on stroking the ball to the picture.

Tiger quickly grasped the concept of putting to the picture. He had an opportunity to show what he had learned when, as a two-year-old, he competed in his first tournament—a pitch, putt, and drive contest at the Navy Golf Course in Cypress. He wasn't the least bit concerned about being by far the youngest child in the ten-and-under age bracket. In fact, I was a lot more nervous than he. Tiger took first place and the trophy that went with it. The putting-to-the-picture system works. It's the same system my son uses today.

Some of the simplest games involve putting. They instill a spirit of competition. Your child will alternately experience the exhilaration of success and the determination to bounce back from failure. Here are some games I hope

Every putt is straight, but the slope of the green forces the ball to move.

you will find instrumental in helping your child develop a positive attitude toward competition.

⅂ Set a ball one foot from the cup on a practice green. Make sure the putt is straight and relatively flat. The object is to sink as many putts consecutively from that spot as possible. The parent keeps count while the child executes the putt and vice versa. One miss—and believe me, you will miss—and your turn ends. Compare scores. The player with the most sinks in a row wins. Don't be surprised if your child beats you. Children are fearless and less likely to succumb to pressure.

⅂ An extension of the short putting game is to move the ball six inches or so farther from the hole on the same line. The same rules apply.

⅂ Circle the hole with four balls. The object is to make each putt, keeping score to see who can make the most. You have one putt from a specific spot, and that's it. Miss it and you forfeit that opportunity.

⅂ Pick three putts of varying distances. The longest may be 40 feet, the next 20 feet, and the last 10 feet. The object is to see who can get the putts closer to the hole. This teaches distance control, which is more important than direction.

⅂ Start with a one-foot putt. After making that putt, move the ball six inches farther from the hole. If that putt is holed, the player can now move the ball six inches farther. But if the putt is missed, the player must move the ball six inches closer. It is a game of stop-and-start whose punitive nature

65

Circle with four balls drill

teaches patience and concentration. Tiger and I have spent many hours on this drill, and, believe me, it has helped us develop the freedom to laugh at each other's miscues as well as admire each other's successes. You might make four straight putts and you're out to three feet, and then you miss four straight and you're back to one foot. It provides an excellent opportunity for your child to see that parents are indeed fallible. It also encourages a repeating putting stroke and teaches your child how to putt under pressure.

Putting is a game of success. You want a mental picture of the ball going into the hole. The more you see that picture, the easier it becomes to putt. This game promotes good-natured ribbing and a sense of accomplishment. "Mommy, the game was over when I got to five feet and Daddy was back at one," Tiger would gleefully report. His pride swelled along with his anticipation of the next showdown between us.

◁ My personal philosophy in putting is that there are no three-putt greens. There is only a poor first putt. That is what I taught Tiger through a game designed to perfect the art of lag putting, which is the stroking of a long putt as close to the hole as possible. "What is the purpose of this putt?" I would ask. "To get it close enough so I have a ho-hum second putt," Tiger would answer. Lag putting is a key to success on the green. Place three balls 25 feet from the hole. The object is to putt those balls as close to the hole as possible, then validate the no-three-putt theory by making the second putt. It teaches the value of making a good first putt.

◁ There are two methods of practice putting. One is to work on developing a repeating stroke with a sound technique, and the other is to practice making putts. There is a big difference between the two. Developing a repeating stroke means focusing on a good, solid, square technical stroke without concern for holing the putt. The other requires concentration on making the putt with the use of this repeating stroke.

The two types of putts are lag putts and make putts. Shown here is an example of a lag putt, the objective of which is to get the ball within a three-foot radius of the hole.

69

Here's a drill: Place the ball one foot from the hole. Put the putter behind the ball, and put a tee at each end of the putter so that the putter barely clears the gap between the tees. This is called the gap drill. The object is to bring the putter back through that gate, creating a square repeating stroke. Bring the putter back through the gap 25 times. Then remove the tees and see how many putts you can make in succession. The pressure increases in proportion to the number of successively holed putts, and you will realize how the human body is affected by pressure. You will also discover how good your repeating stroke is and how long you can maintain it.

Speaking of pressure and its effect on performance, Tiger and I would sometimes end our practice sessions with a competitive drill. This consisted of placing a ball three feet from the hole and seeing how many consecutive putts we could make without missing. Sounds simple, doesn't it? A lousy three-foot putt. Anybody could make those. But believe me, as the number mounts, the pressure increases tremendously. He would start, and then I would wait and wait and wait and wait. After seventy in a row, I would still be standing there. He was that good, and was I ever proud!

Our tradition was to end all practice sessions with a trip to the nineteenth hole. I would say, "Tiger, you are ridiculous. I have had it, let's go into the nineteenth hole for a drink." In Tiger's case it was a cherry coke.

The gap drill

THE SHORT GAME

7

Verbalization, Confidence, Technique, Visualization, Competition

Jack Nicklaus's teacher, Jack Grout, taught him to hit the ball with his driver as far as he could. My philosophy is different; I believe golf should be taught from the green back to the tee, emphasizing putting first. That's the approach I took in teaching Tiger. When he was very young, I told him the last club in his bag that he would master would be his driver. The fact that he occasionally struggled with hitting it accurately as a teenager proves my point.

The reason most teaching professionals emphasize the short game is because that's where strokes are saved. It is not my intention to teach the fundamentals of chipping, pitching, and the golf swing—just a working knowledge so that you can assist your child in the early stages of development. Later, I will touch on when it's time to enlist the services of a professional.

Let the child grip the club any way he or she wants. The principle to teach after a trial period is posture and balance. It is important to teach the proper technique of each phase and to demonstrate the subtle differences between the four phases. In other words, this is a step-by-step progression: putting, chipping, pitching, and the full swing.

Hit it and rip it first and foremost.

Golf is absorbed more easily when learning proceeds from the green back to the tee. Putting is first.

Second, chipping

Third, pitching

Last, but not least, the full swing

Choke down on club at least halfway down the grip.

The proper chipping setup is with the weight on the inside of the left foot.

Chipping

Chipping is the first attempt at ball-striking to the green and is used up to 20 yards away. But before you start, you should develop a preshot procedure that will extend through the full swing. Every shot starts from behind the ball. You must look at the ball and then at the target and get a feel for how far to hit the ball and for the variables: elevation (uphill, downhill, sidehill, and so on), hazards (over a bunker or water), and type of turf (short or long grass, firm or soft soil). Having weighed these factors, you approach the ball, either from the right or the left, take one or two practice swings to get a proper feel, step up to the ball, and then execute the shot with full confidence. This SOP will

Side view from up-target   Side view from down-target

get more complicated the longer the shot becomes because other variables will have to be taken into consideration, but more on that later.

It is easier to visualize a shot from behind the ball than while addressing the ball from either side of the target line. Walk through the SOP with your child, and verbalize factors that you think will affect the shot. Continue as you address the ball, using the putt-to-the-picture technique. Only after it is clear that the child understands the procedure is it time to demonstrate chipping technique.

One of the main differences between chipping and putting is the setup. In chipping, the weight of the body is mostly on the inside of the left foot and remains there throughout the swing. The body should be aligned slightly left of target or open, with the club face pointing at the target line. The feet

Chipping sequence: The length of the shot determines the distance the club is taken back, which in turn determines the length of the follow-through.

Contact is crisp and delivered with a slight descending blow.

should be no more than six inches apart. On most occasions, the stroke is slightly longer than that used for a putt and is delivered with a slightly descending blow. The wrists do not turn over but remain in a locked position in the follow-through after the ball is struck. The head remains in a passive position (stable but not rigid), and the focus should be on

The knees move slightly to the left at impact.

watching the club hit the ball. The shot is executed by a short, crisp downward stroke of the ball, with a brief, abbreviated follow-through. The weight remains inside the left foot for the entire shot. On the follow-through, the head will automatically rotate and follow the ball's flight to the hole. Parents should stress watching the club hit the ball. This pro-

85

motes truer, more solid contact and eliminates problems that occur from excessive body movement.

Remember:

◁ Start from behind the ball.

◁ Identify and verbalize the variables.

◁ Set the weight on the left side.

◁ Look at the target, and then look at the ball, as in putting.

◁ Chip to the picture, making certain to watch the club hit the ball before any movement of the head.

Pitching

The pitch shot is utilized anywhere from 20 to 100 yards from the green, depending upon the size and strength of the golfer. The same principles of chipping apply to pitching—start behind the ball, take into consideration all the factors, hit to the picture, and watch the club hit the ball. Consider the pitch a chip with a longer swing because of the added distance. The basic difference between the two is that unlike the chip, with the weight mostly on the left side, the pitch shot is executed with the weight equally distributed on the inside of each foot. The feet should be spread comfortably apart and the body slightly open to the target line; the club is taken back slowly and smoothly while the weight transfers to the right side (for right-handers). On the downswing the weight flows to the left side as the club descends and strikes the ball, sending it on its

In pitching the feet are spread apart slightly more than in chipping. Weight is balanced equally inside both feet.

The backswing is longer, and the weight is allowed to move to inside right foot.

The weight shifts to left side at impact.

The hands extend toward the target.

The follow-through is high.

way to the target. The follow-through is slightly longer.

There are some additional factors in pitching such as wind, terrain, and lie (how the ball sets on the grass). No change in the swing is necessary to assist the ball up on its flight. One of the truisms in golf is that if you want the ball to go up, you hit down. Never try to scoop the ball or help it in the air.

As with putting and chipping, the parent should walk through the procedure for the pitch shot, verbalizing each step so that the child can use both sight and sound to absorb the information. Stress that the swing should be slow and smooth to produce the feeling of effortless power. This way the child understands that there is no correlation between distance and swinging hard. It is amazing how far a golf ball will go when struck crisply and cleanly, even by a child.

Remember:

⦚ Chipping principles apply.

⦚ Distribute weight evenly and on the inside of each foot.

⦚ Allow weight to transfer to the right side and back to the left (for right-handers).

Here are some chipping and pitching games that will test your child's skills:

⦚ With a piece of chalk, draw a three-foot circle around a hole on the practice green. The object is to chip the ball within that circle. You can increase the complexity of the game by

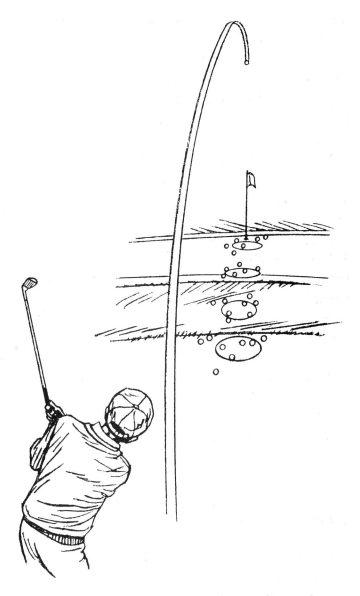

Competitive games are the fun way to learn. Practice, practice, practice.

changing the chip from uphill to downhill. You can also vary the distance the ball must be carried before it lands on the green. For instance, practice chipping over a bunker. This teaches selecting the proper club to propel the ball far enough to reach the green cleanly and then come to rest within the drawn circle. Instead of using a sand wedge, which throws the ball high into the air and makes it land softly, you may opt for a club that produces a lower trajectory to produce a hit-and-roll shot. This is a preferred chipping method because it's a lot easier to control distance when the ball spends more time on the ground than in the air.

It is most important to convey to your child the importance of visualizing a spot where he or she wants the ball to land. The use of a small bucket is helpful. Place the bucket at the desired landing point. Then have your child try to chip the ball into the bucket. Keep count of how many balls the child is able to land in the bucket. You'd be amazed how the percentage increases with practice. This game teaches distance control and spot visualization, and it increases your child's feel around the green.

Because everyone is not fortunate enough to have access to a practice facility, it is often necessary to make the best of what's available. That's where creativity comes in. Parents can use props in their backyard as teaching aids. Place a small tub two-thirds filled with water about 30 feet away from the chipping area. I would suggest the use of an artificial grass mat from which to chip as a way to preserve

Parents participate in the practice of short-game skills.

your lawn. The object is to chip the ball into the tub. It is more difficult than it sounds because the ball must enter the tub at the proper angle or it will skip out. This game also teaches distance control and trajectory.

◁ Establish three or more targets, each at a different distance from your child. They should not be in a progression of close, intermediate, far, and farther, but rather mixed: close, far, intermediate, farther. This requires concentration on distance on each separate shot.

When Tiger was competing in his first golf tournament, as previously mentioned, he was able to hit the ball 80 yards with his 2.5-wood. He could accurately hit a pitch shot 30–40 yards. He was only two, and word of his golfing exploits spread quickly around Southern California. Jim Hill, a reporter for local CBS affiliate KCBS, did the first television feature story on Tiger. He and his cameraman followed Tiger as he played the first hole—a 405-yard par–4—at the Navy course. I had assigned a par of 7 for Tiger because I determined he would need five full shots to get to the green and then two putts to complete the hole. I was correct. He reached the hole in five shots and had a 25-footer for birdie. The camera operator placed his camera behind the hole and, in the true spirit of television, Hill said, "Sink it, Tiger." The resulting putt traveled halfway to the hole and stopped. I couldn't understand what happened because I knew Tiger was putting to the picture and was a much better putter than he displayed. Hill told Tiger to give it another try. Again, the ball traveled halfway to the hole and stopped. This time I knew something was wrong, so I asked the cameraman to move his camera to the side. Tiger stroked the putt a third time. It rolled beautifully, right on line, and stopped a couple of inches from the hole. He didn't want to break the camera.

THE FULL SWING

8

Maximizing the Mind, Paralysis/Analysis, Patience, Understanding

The full swing is simply an extension of the pitch, employing a longer arc. The same fundamentals apply: grip of choice, feet comfortably apart, and the knowledge that in order to hit the ball farther the swing must be longer. Stress taking the club back slowly and watching the club hit the ball. Do not make it any more complicated than that. Tell your child that the golf swing is nothing more than opening the door and closing the door. You open the door on the backswing and close it on the downswing. If you want to hit the ball harder, you open the door and slam the door shut. This conveys a visual picture of the realities of the golf swing.

Another swing thought is, "turn, turn." This idea reduces

This is the golf swing in its simplest form. Open the door, close the door. The golf swing starts with the upper body rotating away from the ball. The rotation back provides the power and direction. Turn, turn.

the full swing to its ultimate simplicity. You turn away from the ball then back toward the ball. Both of these thoughts should greatly assist your child in visualizing what occurs in a full golf swing without being encumbered by reams of technical details. I'm sure you have heard of paralysis by analysis, which occurs when the mind becomes overloaded with the complexities of the golf swing and thereby impairs performance. The conscious mind is usually in control of our activities, but it is too slow to guide the golf swing. It is the subconscious that actually swings the golf club.

To understand how this works, try to remember how you

All shots begin behind the ball. Pick a spot in front of the ball to aim the club face.

Align the club face with the chosen spot in front of the ball.

After aligning your body with the club face, rotate your head to verify the correct aim and alignment. Waggle the club.

You are now properly aimed, aligned, and in a solid setup ready to hit a powerful, accurate golf shot.

first learned how to drive a car, especially if you were learning with a manual shift. Your reactions were very mechanical and slow. The sequence went something like this: push in the clutch; shift the gears; let out the clutch; press the accelerator; and at the same time, steer the car. It wasn't easy. Now, years later, driving becomes second nature to you. You don't even think about it.

The golf swing is the same way. Trouble occurs when the conscious mind is activated during the swing. The conscious mind should be active only during the preshot routine and the analysis of factors that will affect the shot: wind, elevation, lie, and so on. There is a way to harmonize the workings of the conscious and subconscious parts of the mind, but it's easier said than done. That is why I strongly recommend the simplest possible approach to the full swing. If you don't clutter your conscious mind with endless pointers before swinging, you will make it easier for your subconscious instincts to guide you.

Don't forget that the swing is built from the green back to the tee. With proper training, practice, and dedication, 95 percent of the golf swing will be in place before your child ever takes a full swing. That is the optimum. But your child will be swinging long before approaching that ideal. What can you do to prevent your child from developing a bad golf swing? Constantly encourage your child to practice the short game—chipping and pitching. This will require tremendous patience and understanding on your part because the natural instinct is to hit the ball as hard and as far as you can.

Tiger took a different path to the full swing. When Tiger

The full swing begins with a proper setup and alignment. Waggle to reduce tension.

On the backswing, when the club is parallel to the ground, the toe of the club should be vertical.

At the top, the club is parallel to the ground and pointed left of the target line.

On the downswing, weight transfers to the right side. The left arm remains straight.

With the weight fully transferred, the hands are releasing to square up the club face.

The hands have released.

Both arms are straight after impact.

The follow-through is high.

The body is in perfect balance.

Finish with the navel pointing straight at the target. "Good swing!"

sat in his high chair in the garage and watched me hit balls into the net, he was assimilating and learning how to execute the full swing. It was like a movie being run over and over and over for his view. The result was that he learned the full swing before he learned to chip and putt. In fact, one day, when he was ten months old, I unstrapped him from the high chair while I took a break from my practice. He toddled over to his little putter, walked over to my hitting area, selected a ball, set up, and hit the ball into the net. I was so flabbergasted that I almost fell out of the chair. I ran to get his mother. We came back into the garage, and Tiger had calmly selected another ball and was doing just what his Dad did, except that he was doing it left-handed. It took him two weeks to realize that Dad was not on this side of the ball—he was on the other side. So, one day, in the middle of his swing, he abruptly stopped, walked around on the other side of the ball, changed his grip to a right-hand grip, and hit the ball as if nothing had happened. I knew then that I had something special because I had never said anything about changing the grip from left-handed to right-handed. It was an instinctive athletic move.

Tiger's swing underwent continuous development under the auspices of subsequent professional instruction. Your child could experience the same developmental process.

Remember:

◁ The full swing is merely an extension of pitching.
◁ Keep it simple.
◁ Open the door, close the door.
◁ Turn, turn.

115

Each subsequent photo in this series illustrates a checkpoint you can use to review your child's swing.

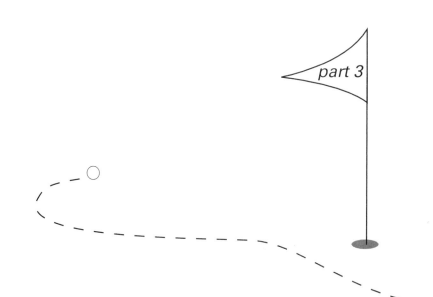

part 3

What It Takes to Play the Game

PRACTICE

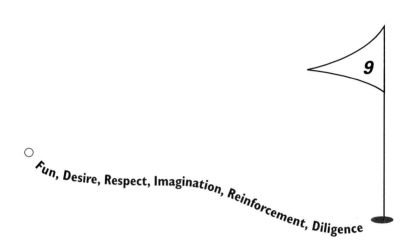

9

Fun, Desire, Respect, Imagination, Reinforcement, Diligence

You get out of golf what you put into it. There are no short-cuts. Introducing the fundamentals of the game to your child is only the beginning of the journey to success. Practice is necessary to make the ride as smooth as possi-ble. The late great teacher Harvey Penick once wrote, "Practicing is an individual matter. . . . Whatever the child wants to do—play or practice—that's what he or she should do." I totally agree, but I must reiterate that only through practice will your child reach his or her full poten-tial in the game. Practice should be fun. It should be inter-esting and varied. And, above all, it should be competitive.

When Tiger was two years old, he memorized my work telephone number. Each afternoon, about an hour before quitting time, he would call and say, "Daddy, can I practice with you today?" I would pause an inordinate length of time, just long enough to engender the fear that Daddy was going to say no. I would, of course, say, yes. Then he would say, "OK, Daddy, I'll meet you at the golf course. I'll have Mom bring me over!" The desire to practice must come from the child. One of the things that I pride myself on is that I have never, in Tiger's entire life, asked him to practice or told him to practice. The motivation must come from within. And this is established by the rapport, the respect, and love for the game that you communicate to your child.

Tiger: "Daddy, can I practice with you today?"
Dad: "Mmmmm. OK."

There is practice and good practice. Every practice session must have a purpose. You just don't go out to the course and get on the driving range and blindly bang balls. There should be an order to the practice session. Set up a practice station by laying down three clubs: one pointing at the target on the far side of the ball, one parallel to the target line and in front of the toes, and the other 90 degrees to the target line, extending between the feet. This will give the child a lesson in alignment and target awareness. The club pointing at the target properly aligns the body and shoulders left of the target. The club parallel to the target line provides directional reinforcement of the club face, which points to the target, and the body, which points to the left of the target. The club between the feet provides a fix on ball position within the stance. The child will quickly learn that the shorter irons set up square to the target when played closer to the right foot and that longer irons and woods naturally fall more toward the left foot. What you have established here is that each club, with its unique construction, dictates a different ball location in the setup. I know that some claim that there should be one ball position for all clubs, but that isn't natural. It requires too much leg drive to achieve solid contact. The method I use is natural and instinctive and thus can be easily assimilated by your child.

This is a typical organization of a work station at the driving range.

You as parents can assist your child by checking alignment and aim. Don't forget a sound, athletic setup!

After those plaintive phone calls from little Tiger, I would take him to the golf course almost daily. He would set up his work station and begin hitting balls. The first question I would always ask him was, "What is your target?"

He would reply, "That palm tree on the end of the driving range."

I would ask, "What palm tree?"

He would say, "That third one from the left." What he was doing was correct. Each shot that you hit in your entire life must have a target, or it is a wasted effort. Never hit a shot without a target. Why? The human body, in this natural approach to golf, must always have something to focus on, the more specific the better.

Don't oversupervise. Let the child play. Let the child's imagination come to the forefront. I suggest that each ball be placed on a tee to help ensure that the child makes solid contact, thereby building confidence and promoting enjoyment of the practice session. The parent should be as unobtrusive as possible. Set up your own work station and work on your game. If you see an area where you can help, by all means make suggestions. Avoid criticism. Never make negative comments. Positive reinforcement is much more effective. For example: "I think you would hit the ball better if you played the ball a little bit more toward your right foot." Suggest, don't dictate. Both you and your child are out there to have fun first. While you are having fun, you are learning about the golf swing. Also while you're there, to keep it interesting, you should be competitive. "What's your target?"

"The 50-yard sign out there."

"OK, I bet I can get it closer to the 50-yard sign than you."

"OK, ten balls."

Whoever gets the most balls closer is the winner. This is pure competition. There is no reward other than the satisfaction of winning. Don't encourage your child to bet. Competition is enough.

The target should be as specific as possible—one flag of three. Each golf swing during practice should have a target. A practice work station should be used during every session. This reinforces proper alignment and ball position.

You can vary the targets and the game—three balls, five balls, and so on. Let your imagination be your guide. As a parent, you're there to reinforce several things:

◁ Alignment

◁ Swing

◁ Target for Each Shot

◁ Fun

◁ Competition

Work stations can also be set up in bunkers to practice sand play. Proper technique is demonstrated above: feet open to target line; weight on left side; arms hanging with club laid open. Keep head motionless.

136

After a slow backswing, aim the clubface to enter the sand three to four inches behind the ball. Do not try to "help" the ball up, the sand itself will do this.

Follow-through consistent with the length of backswing and the distance you want the ball to fly.

Maintain balance.

As your child gets older and more proficient, you should encourage "working" the ball. By that I mean hitting the ball deliberately from right to left or left to right, high, low, under the wind—using a variety of skills to cause the ball to arrive at a single target by different methods and directions. This the first step toward creating a shot maker—controlling the flight and direction of the ball on call.

Tiger was always fascinated by my 1-iron when he was little, and he always tried to swing it. But because of the length and loft, he could only dribble it on the ground. The club was longer than he was. But he said to me, "Someday Daddy, I'm going to be able to hit this club." And I said to him, "Son, someday you are going to be one of the best in the world at long-iron play. This 1-iron is your friend. It will always be your friend."

Later, as he grew and we began to play shot maker, working the ball right to left, he developed the ability to hit the 1-iron. Aiming at the driving range fence, he would hit the ball over the perimeter fence that separates the range from the golf course, make the ball turn from right to left, come back over the fence, and land in the middle of the driving range. He called that his "deliberate hook." He used this shot in the 1994 U.S. Amateur in his comeback by hooking the ball low while in the trees and landing it on the fairway, where it rolled up onto the green—to the chagrin of his opponent. Champions are made on the driving range. Practice, practice, practice. If, at the end of each practice, you can walk away from the range holding each other's hand and arguing about who won the most, believe me, it is a warm, wonderful feeling.

Other ways to assist your child in swing development and practice

Hold club lightly and assist in a "one-piece" takeaway.

141

Your grip ensures child's takeaway is on the correct path. Notice there has been *no* movement of the hands to this point.

Assist your child in achieving a correct position at the top. Club should be parallel to the target line and ground (on a full swing with the driver). Repeat until the correct position is accomplished several times.

Position at the top has club parallel to the target line and ground.
Note shadow of the shaft is vertical, indicating both have been
achieved.

THINKING WHILE YOU PLAY

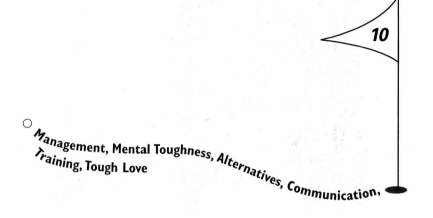

10

Management, Mental Toughness, Alternatives, Communication, Training, Tough Love

I promised myself when Tiger was two years old that I would make two contributions to his golf game: course management and mental toughness, the latter an outgrowth of my upbringing and my years as a Green Beret.

What is course management? Simply put, it is the way you manage and conduct your game on the golf course. Do you walk up to the ball and just hit it? Or do you reflect for a moment, look around, and determine that there are other factors affecting your shot, such as wind, lie, target, and thickness of the grass? All these factors result in an evaluation that must take place even before club selection.

Here's how I introduced Tiger to course management. One day, when Tiger was two, we were on the second hole at Navy Golf Course. He had hit his ball into the trees to the right on a short par–4. I said, "What are you going to do, Tiger?" He looked and he said, "I can't hit the ball over these trees, Daddy, they're too tall."

"Well, what else are you going to do?" I asked.

"I can hit it between those trees, but I've got to keep it down. And there's a big sand twap."

"OK, what else can you do?"

He looked to the left and said, "I can hit my ball out into the fairway, hit my next shot onto the green, and one-putt for a par."

I said, "Son, that is course management." He had identified and evaluated his alternatives and chosen the one most likely to be successful.

So you see, you don't have to be a genius. All you have to do is use common sense and try to do the best you can, and on every shot take the best opportunity for success after considering all the factors that go into a successful shot.

An important part of course management is knowing in advance what you plan to do on each hole. This is called a game plan. During the practice rounds of tournaments, Tiger and I will each prepare a plan of attack on every hole. This includes an evaluation of the degree of difficulty of the hole, which club to use for the tee shot, where you want to put that shot, and other factors as they become apparent. At the conclusion of the round, we would sit down and compare notes. For instance, on the first hole—a 420-yard par–4—my game plan could call for him to hit a driver down the right side of the fairway with a draw to avoid the left fairway bunker. It also positions the ball to approach the green from the right side because there is a huge bunker on the left side. His plan might call for a 3-wood down the right side with a short- to middle-iron to the green. After discussion he would adopt either plan or a mutually agreed upon compromise.

Course management dictates that if the wind is behind you, then you probably would use a 3-wood. But if the wind is in your face, you would need the driver. And the resultant second shot would also be affected. But the principle is the same: Have a plan on how you're going to play a specific hole before you even get there. That's the point. It allows you the luxury of not having to make every decision on each while on the tee. Now you have the comfort of minor adjustments. This is repeated on every hole, including par–3s.

A game plan is not productive unless you stick to it.

In the summer of Tiger's twelfth year, he played in the Southern California Junior Golf Association Match Play Championship. While following him, I observed that he was two up by virtue of having made two birdies in the first four holes. On the fifth hole his opponent, who had won the previous hole, took his driver and hit it into the left woods. Tiger reached for his driver and promptly hit his into the right woods. I asked myself, "What is he doing?" At the conclusion of the match, which Tiger won four and three, I asked him, "Why did you hit your driver on the fifth hole after your opponent was in the woods?"

And he answered, "I was two under par, and I wanted to get to three under."

I said, "Son, that's not the way to play match play."

And in his infinite wisdom, he looked me in the eye and innocently said, "Dad, you haven't taught me how to play match play."

And I hadn't. So I said, "Son, this fall I will put you through Woods's Finishing School."

He said, "Good." Little did he know what he was in for.

My plan was to put Tiger through some rigorous training in mental toughness. But before we began, I thought it was necessary to establish some ground rules. They were as follows: If at any time he wanted the training to end, he would just mention a code word that we had, and the training would be over; second, there were no other rules—everything goes, and he could say nothing in response.

Course management is thinking your way around the golf course. Plan before executing.

This plan might not be effective with every child. You must know your child's disposition and tolerance level. The sort of training that I put Tiger through might be counterproductive and alienate your child. So I do not recommend it for every parent. Tiger and I have a very strong personal relationship based upon mutual trust and respect developed over the years. That is the only way I would have considered putting him through this kind of training.

With Tiger there was never any guesswork. I knew him and how much he could take. So I pulled every nasty, dirty, rambunctious, obnoxious trick on my son week after week after week. I dropped a bag of clubs at impact of his swing. I imitated a crow's voice while he was stroking a putt. When he was about ready to hit a shot, I would toss a ball right in front of his, and it would cross his line of vision. I would make sure that I stood in his line of sight and would move just as he was about to execute the shot. I would cough as he was taking the club back. I would say, "Don't hit it in the water." Those were the *nice* things I did. In other words, I played with his mind. And don't forget, he was not permitted to say a word.

Sometimes he got so angry with me that he would stop his club on the downswing inches before impact, turn, and glare at me because I had dropped a set of clubs on the ground. He would grit his teeth and roll his eyes, and the only response he got was, "Don't look at me. Are you going to hit the ball or not?"

I taught him every little trick that an opponent could possibly pull on him in match play, and some that I invented myself. I even—and I'm not proud of this—cheated, just to get a reaction from him. Because let's face it, somewhere down the line, somebody was going to do that to him. How do you cheat? Well, I would mark my ball on a putt with my right hand, but I would leave the coin with my left, two feet closer to the hole. And he knew I was cheating, but remember, he wasn't permitted to say anything.

During finishing school, Tiger was exposed to every devious, diabolical, insidious trick that any future opponent could pull on him. And not once did he utter the code word. He later told me it was the most difficult experience of his entire life. At times, he was so angry with me he wanted to destroy his clubs. He never forgot that this was for his benefit alone. But he certainly wouldn't have wished this training on any other human being. I must admit it was equally tough on me. Some of the things I did didn't fill me with pride and joy either.

But he learned. And he became mentally tough. Later I assured him that in his entire life, no opponent would be as mentally tough as he, ever! The results are a 36–3 match play record in United States Golf Association championships, three consecutive USGA Junior titles, and three straight U.S. Amateur championships. He has won on the eighteenth hole. He has won on the nineteenth hole. He has come back from six holes down to win. And it is all the fruit of his mental toughness.

ETIQUETTE, CUSTOMS AND TRADITIONS, RULES AND REGULATIONS

11

Acceptable and Unacceptable Conduct, Integrity, Knowledge, Conformity, Compliance, Honesty

Each sport has unwritten rules of etiquette that informally define acceptable and unacceptable behavior. For example, in basketball it is a normal practice for members of the audience to do everything in their power to distract the visiting player while shooting a free throw. In golf, however, similar conduct would be intolerable. To assist you in teaching your child how not to embarrass himself on the course, I have identified some of the rules of etiquette as follows:

⫪ Never run on the putting green.

⫪ Never step on another player's direct line to the hole.

151

⅂ Stand still and remain quiet while another player is executing a shot.

⅂ Always be ready to hit when it's your turn.

⅂ Stay out of the peripheral vision of another golfer when he or she is readying or hitting the ball.

⅂ Repair your ball mark and others when on the putting surface. Always leave the course in better shape than you found it.

⅂ Identify your ball with a distinctive marking.

⅂ Avoid slow play. Keep up with the group in front of you, not in front of the group behind you.

⅂ Always shake the hand of your opponent or playing companion at the end of a round of golf.

⅂ Always yell "Fore!" if your shot potentially endangers others.

⅂ If you hear "Fore!" cover your head; don't run.

⅂ In golf you have one shot; there are no mulligans (second chances).

⅂ Take one or two practice swings only.

⅂ Avoid lost balls by following their flight to a conclusion. Mark the ball with a landmark or natural object (for example, a tree, bush, or mound) to make it easier to locate.

⅂ If you're playing slowly, allow the following group to play through.

⅂ Replace all divots.

⌐ Rake the bunkers.

⌐ Keep all equipment off the green.

⌐ When all players are finished on the green, replace the flagstick carefully to avoid damage to the edges of the cup.

⌐ Leave the green immediately, and mark your score later.

⌐ Never throw a club.

⌐ Congratulate playing companions on a shot well executed. Be a good sport and enjoy the game.

Golf is the only nonofficiated sport we have. You are expected to call a penalty on yourself if you break the rules. It's important that parents communicate the importance of integrity and honesty because that is the heart and soul of the game.

The rules of golf are based upon integrity and gentlemanly conduct, with a dash of common sense. If you follow them, your enjoyment of the game will be enhanced immeasurably. It would be counterproductive for me to reproduce the rules of golf on these pages. But here are a few examples:

⌐ The person whose ball is farthest from the hole shoots first.

⌐ Always mark your ball position on the green with a coin or suitable item. Place the coin immediately behind the ball on the part of the ball farthest from the hole.

⌐ The proper procedure for offsetting your ball is to mark your ball and then line your putter head up with an identifiable object from your marker on the ground. Pick up your marker and move it to the other extremity of the putter head. There's only one correct way to do this, and don't forget to use the reverse procedure when it is your turn to putt. Never offset from the ball, always from your marker.

◁ If you hit your ball in an area designated as out of bounds, you must play a second ball from the original spot. You incur a stroke and distance penalty. In other words, you are hitting plus two.

Understanding, appreciation, and knowledge of the etiquette, customs, rules, and regulations of golf will greatly facilitate and enhance your child's enjoyment of the game and life.

IT'S TOURNAMENT TIME

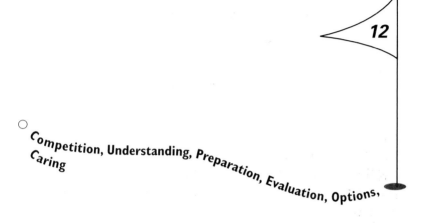

12

Competition, Understanding, Preparation, Evaluation, Options, Caring

Now you've created a monster—a competitive eager monster who wants to strut his stuff. Mom, Pop, I've got news for you: Your child doesn't need you as much anymore. What is desired most now is the big "C" (competition). Sure, you have spent the last X number of years working diligently to develop those talents, but the proof is in the pudding and in competition with other golfers.

It's not a reflection on you. It's the need for the bird to exercise his wings and fly from the nest. How do you know it's time? There is no single best time. It isn't necessary for you to know: Your child will know. And like any proud mother and father bird, you should acknowledge it and encourage it when the time comes.

This time came so rapidly with Tiger that I was almost caught unprepared—almost. Due to my socioeconomic status, I knew in advance that I could not join a country club. I had, therefore, made alternative plans. What was the best way for a middle-class parent to create an opportunity for his child to play golf on some of the best courses in Southern California? The answer was a junior golf association.

Fortunately for us, the Southern California area was home to one of the best junior golf programs in the world—the Southern California Junior Golf Association. The organization sponsored one-day tournaments during the summer months four or five times per week at some of the most exclusive country clubs. This fit perfectly into my master game plan for Tiger to grow up and develop on the highest-caliber golf courses.

At the age of four, my little man joined the SCJGA. The

Members of the Heartwell Golf Course Junior Club await their weekly Saturday tee time.

Tiger tees it up at the Optimist International Junior World in San Diego, California.

youngest age bracket was ten-and-under, and there he competed with no handicap against children far older than he. About the same time, he was kicked off the Navy Golf Course for being too young, even after receiving certification for play by three PGA head professionals. So he joined the junior golf association of Heartwell Golf Park in Long Beach. This also permitted him to play a tournament there each Saturday of the year. It was an extension of the tournaments offered by the SCJGA, which played Monday through Friday during the summer months only.

It took Tiger all of four tournaments to win his first nine-holer. It was at Yorba Linda Country Club, and he was ecstatic. The young man he beat was ten years old and had a very difficult time accepting defeat. Tiger took winning as

157

a given. The little guy just knew intuitively how good he was. This was the first of many triumphs in both organizations.

Research your area and determine what organizations and what facilities are available for your child's use. If you are a member of a country club, your needs are probably already met, but for nonclub members it's imperative that you know your options in advance. Have the information and application on hand when your child communicates his readiness. To whom do you talk? Where do you go?

A proud Southern California Junior Golf Association warrior accepts his first-place eight-and-under age division trophy at Knollwood Golf Course.

You won't find the answers in the yellow pages. You have to do the leg work yourself: Talk to the PGA professionals in your city and obtain the information on any junior golf clubs or organizations functioning therein, get the application, fill it out, have the check ready, and go when the time comes.

A media veteran at five

Each city has different organizations. What you look for is a well-organized, well-funded, responsible, caring organization with competition in the age brackets consistent with your child's age. Never force your child to compete in an age bracket too advanced for his physical development. Tiger was an exception. The psyche of a child is a fragile thing. No child wants to get his brains beat in consistently. He at least wants to have a fair chance of winning. So if the organization doesn't have a ten-and-under age bracket competition and your child is six years old, don't put him in with the eleven-year-olds, because it could cause irreparable or unnecessary damage to your child as a person and a golfer. Use common sense. Follow your instincts. You will naturally do the best you can. If you have a problem, seek help. There may be other parents in your community that have experience and information.

There are numerous ways parents can participate.

Sometimes early departures for tournaments are
tough on both parent and child.

Earlier I said that bringing up your child is a joint and
family effort. Golf is no exception. When Tiger started playing competitively at age four, my wife was ready, too. Just
like any other little-league mother, she entered him and
chauffeured him to all the tournaments during the summer.
I can still remember cracking one eye at 4:00 A.M. when she
and Tiger were preparing to leave for a nine-hole tournament a 90-minute drive away. He never complained when
the alarm went off. He got up like a little trooper, brushed
his teeth, washed his face and hands, dressed himself, and
prepared to do battle. The last thing I heard as I dozed off
to sleep was, "Tiger, don't forget your pillow so you can
sleep in the car."

Mom thought of everything. She became the chief cook

161

and bottle washer. Was she ever involved in junior golf! She was the official scorekeeper, head cheerleader, and rules interpreter for any group Tiger found himself in. I must give her credit: She was impartial in her cheerleading but seemed a little harder on Tiger when he inevitably goofed up. "Tiger, what you doing?" she would say with cool.

In junior golf parents are not permitted to talk to their children during competition, but to her that rule was for everybody else, especially when it came to her son. In fairness, she was equally supportive of all the players. She wasn't belligerent or disruptive, and the kids respected and loved her totally. Kids always know when someone cares and is for real.

Mom discharged her yeoman duties quite admirably until Tiger reached the age of thirteen. I had anticipated his development and planned my early retirement from McDonnell Douglas, after which I took over the responsibilities of taking Tiger to tournaments—not local but national. To ensure that he was not entered in tournaments

Tiger meets Jack Nicklaus at Belaire Country Club in Los Angeles during a clinic.

over his head, I gave him one major national tournament of his choosing. He selected the Big I (Independent Insurance Agents of America Golf Tournament). The choice to allow him to advance to the national level was easy for me because Tiger had clearly demonstrated his superiority over local talent in his age group. In fact, he was undefeated as a twelve-year-old.

Your author takes a break from a hectic tournament day.

Your choice may not be as easy or readily apparent. Have your child evaluated by a reputable PGA teaching pro whom you trust before making a commitment to advanced national competition. You see, local competition extends by age group all the way to the eighteenth birthday, so you have ample time. The point is that your child should not be forced into a level of competition for which he or she isn't physically or mentally prepared. There's plenty of time.

There are several organizations that can be joined for competition at the national level. First and foremost is the American Junior Golf Association, which has age brackets of thirteen to fourteen and fifteen to eighteen. This organization extends the age limit for junior golf to the nineteenth birthday to provide an opportunity for its membership to play up to the point that they enter college. The AJGA is organized for the purpose of providing its members competition at the national level and exposure to golf coaches at most of the country's major universities as well as smaller colleges.

Golf camps and clinics are also available to assist your child in refining his or her game and preparing for competition. Some offer scholarships to help parents defray expenses. *Golf Digest* magazine annually publishes a comprehensive list of junior camps and clinics for every region in the United States. The 1996 listing appeared in the magazine's April issue and may be obtained by calling 800-PAR-GOLF.

There is also a myriad of junior golf organizations around the country. One in particular, geared toward minorities and the underprivileged, is the Ladies Golf Professional Tour's junior golf program. This program began in Los Angeles and has expanded into Portland, Detroit, and Wilmington. The number to call for more information about this program and the association's Girls Golf Club and Junior Clinics program is 904–254–8800.

More junior golf programs are springing up every day. And there is surely one in your area. But you have to be vigilant and check them out carefully before considering your child for enrollment.

Becoming a member of the AJGA is simple. Call the headquarters at 770-998-4653 and request a membership application. Fill it out. Membership fee is $70 per year. There is also a $95 fee for entering each tournament. Tournament acceptance involves a selection process by an AJGA competition committee. There are also qualifiers (one-day qualifying tournaments) to give those who do not gain entrance into the tournament field an opportunity to do so. The AJGA is currently planning to establish regional two-day tournaments beyond the normal AJGA tournaments. The United States will be divided into five regions, thus affording opportunities for entrance with minimal travel. Additional information about the AJGA may be obtained by writing to this address: AJGA, 2415, Steeplechase Lane, Roswell, Georgia 30076.

Tiger's development through competition in the AJGA resulted in numerous victories, selection four consecutive years as a first-team All-American, and two Rolex AJGA Player of the Year awards. His success at the national level brought him to the attention of collegiate coaches and resulted in a golf scholarship to Stanford University.

I knew it was time for Tiger to move on to the amateur level of competition when he played his last AJGA tournament in Castle Rock, Colorado. His scores were atrocious. His attitude was indifferent. His approach was sloppy. And he just went through the motions for the first time. His competitive instincts were gone. I knew then that he had outgrown the AJGA. It was time to move on.

The 1993 U.S. Golf Association National champion proudly holds his trophy.

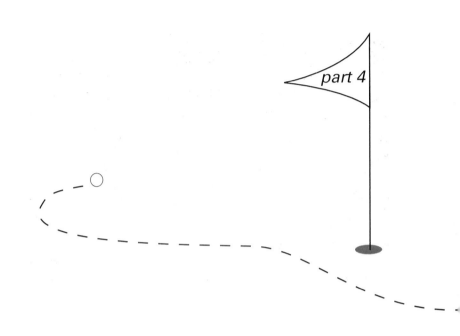

Letting Them Go

WHEN IT'S TIME TO SEEK HELP

13

Guidance, Objectivity, Knowledge, Understanding, Assistance, Perseverance

I have already admitted that I am not a PGA teaching pro. This book is not a panacea or a fully detailed lesson on the golf swing. There are others who are far more qualified than I to teach the golf swing. The fact that you and I are not professionals does not necessarily disqualify us as early coaches for our aspiring young champions. You should evaluate yourself to determine how knowledgeable you are and when it is appropriate to turn your child over to a PGA teaching pro. Be honest and objective. Seeking professional help is not an indication of failure but rather an acknowledgment of what it takes to be successful. The next step is to see that you have taken your child as far as you can on your own. Does this mean the end of your participation?

No. It's just the next step in your child's development and should be a wonderful learning experience for both of you.

That's why it's important to select a professional who is compatible with your personality, your child's personality, and the methodology that you have been teaching your child. Look around. Inquire. Check with other parents. Check with other golfers. Contact your local PGA chapter for recommendations. And don't get just one name, get several. Then interview them. After all, you are turning over to this person one of your most cherished possessions, your child.

When Tiger was four, I realized that he was so talented that he needed the services of a professional to accelerate his development. So I turned him over to Rudy Duran, the head pro at Heartwell Golf Park. Rudy was an affable former PGA Tour player who had a reputation as an excellent teacher with a devout interest in junior golf. Paramount in the selection of Tiger's mentor was my decision to stand in the background and let the two develop a working relationship. Support is much more productive than interference.

Rudy worked with Tiger on the technical aspects of the golf swing and reinforced the early lessons I had taught. Their relationship was one of mutual respect and admiration. Six years later Rudy obtained a new position in Atescadero at Chalk Mountain Golf Club. Although I had been totally involved in Tiger's golf education, Rudy's departure left a big void.

Through the years I had developed contacts and established relationships with numerous PGA teaching professionals at the top country clubs in Southern California. This was made possible by Tiger's participation in the Southern California Junior Golf Association tournaments hosted by these clubs' respective head pros. I contacted each one that I could think of and explained the situation. They all knew Tiger and his proficiency, and one name consistently came up as the first choice: John Anselmo, head teaching pro at Meadowlark Golf Course in Huntington Beach, California.

The USGA National Amateur Trophy

Tiger receives the key to the city of Cypress, California, at a
victory celebration hosted by the city to honor his 1994 U.S.
Amateur Championship.

Before the "wall of fame" Tiger shares his National Amateur Championship trophy with his high school golf coach, Don Crosby.

One of my pro friends, Ray Oakes, was so excited about the prospect of John being Tiger's next teacher that he volunteered to serve as intermediary and contacted John himself to discuss the proposition. He subsequently arranged a meeting between John and me. Since I already had the utmost respect for John and his teaching methods, it was not a difficult decision to tentatively accept him as Tiger's next pro.

However, parents, don't forget that this is not your pro, it's your child's teaching pro. So the next step was to get Tiger's concurrence. He, too, knew John very well, and easily accepted him as his next teacher. They formed a wonderful bond, and John taught him from the age of ten to the age of eighteen. Tiger now works with the Houston-based superteacher Butch Harmon, whose expertise has benefited several touring pros, including Greg Norman. The chemistry between Butch and Tiger was immediate and manifested itself in one of Tiger's greatest shots.

The scene was the hundredth anniversary of the U.S. Amateur at Newport Country Club in Newport, Rhode Island. As defending champion, Tiger had fought off some tough challengers to make it to the final. He and I, as was our custom, had evaluated his game and agreed that if he had a weakness, it was in his ability to control the distance of his mid-short irons. Butch and Tiger had worked to correct the problem, and it was starting to pay dividends, but Tiger was still having a difficult time trusting a change suggested by Butch earlier that week. In the championship match, clinging to a one-up lead over his opponent at the thirty-sixth hole, Tiger faced his moment of truth: an approach shot of 140 yards to an elevated green. His trust in Butch and faith in his own ability enabled him to execute the shot perfectly in the heat of battle. The ball rocketed true off his 8-iron, landed some 15 feet behind the hole and spun back within inches of the cup. Victory was the result of a shot he had learned from Butch just days before and had never attempted in competition.

True champions perform under pressure and in the clutch.

Butch and Tiger had a special celebration between teacher and pupil. But they were not alone. The win surely brought a proud smile from Tiger's early mentors, who had a hand in the development of a champion and his great moment.

WHEN OPPORTUNITY KNOCKS

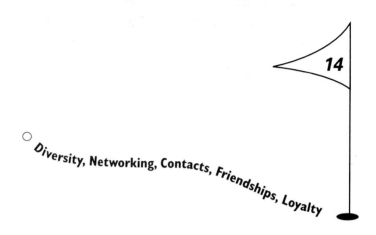

14

Diversity, Networking, Contacts, Friendships, Loyalty

Golf is a microcosm of life. It provides the opportunity for personal and, if you wish, socioeconomic development. What other game can you play where one member of your group is a plumber, another a doctor, and another a chief executive officer of a major corporation? Nowhere else in competitive athletics could this diverse group be assembled and interact. The plumber repaired your broken water heater last week. The doctor delivered your second child one month ago. And the CEO provides your job. Wow! These opportunities exist not only for people like Tiger but also for your child.

In his high school playing days Tiger met one young man who is now a premed student at University of San Diego.

There are many different types of people with varying occupations on the golf course.

He will likely be Tiger's doctor. Another is attending a university to become a lawyer. Need I say Tiger's legal needs will likely be met in the future by this young man?

Your child may well enjoy similar benefits from playing golf. You see, golf is a game for everyone. It knows no social or economic boundaries. And competition can take place between the skilled and the less skilled through the handicap system instituted by the USGA to provide an equal playing field for all. Friendships are born, nurtured, and cemented. Your child has embarked on a beautiful journey. There is no beginning and no ending. Just enjoyment.

Just as important as making contacts is maintaining them. Encourage your child to exchange telephone numbers and addresses. The potential for networking while accompanying your child to tournaments is endless. Keep a record of the contacts you make. They will prove invaluable in the future. Some of the generous people who have provided accommodations for Tiger and me in junior and amateur golf have become our good friends. Even now when I travel to those cities on business or to attend golf tournaments, they roll out the welcome mat. Many have kept up with Tiger's progress and regularly call to see how he's doing. They are our extended family.

If your child shows the kind of dedication it takes to succeed as a competitor in this game, the experience gained and contacts made during junior golf might prove instrumental in securing a college scholarship. What parent doesn't welcome the opportunity to receive some financial relief from the spiraling cost of a college education? Yes, golf can provide or enhance the opportunity for your child to go to college.

One of the most valuable sources of information about collegiate golf is the American College Golf Guide. This paperback book, compiled yearly by the Karsten Manufacturing Corporation, not only addresses junior golf but also lists alphabetically, by state, four-year and two-year colleges with golf programs. Also provided are the coaches' names, addresses, and telephone numbers, and whether or not they conduct junior camps. It contains sample letters and resumes, plus a rating chart to assist parents in comparing prospective colleges. This volume was helpful when our family began researching the college scholarship offers Tiger received during his senior year of high school. But just as important were the contacts we made at places far from home. For additional information about the book, write to this address: Dean Frischknecht Publishing, P.O. Box 1179, Hillsboro, Oregon 97123; the telephone number is 503-648-1333.

As I mentioned earlier, Tiger's first national major tournament was the Big I, held in Texarkana, Arkansas. This tournament has a unique format in that after the thirty-sixth-hole cut, they bring in PGA tour players to match up with three competitors to enable them to play a round of golf with a pro. At thirteen, Tiger's pro was John Daly, then an unknown. I succinctly recall that Tiger was impressed with how far this pro could hit the ball. I passed it off as the imagination of a starry-eyed teenager. But I was wrong. Tiger told me about a shot that Daly hit with a 2-iron that would go 200 yards dead straight and then make an abrupt left turn. He called it his "knot" shot because he compressed the ball so greatly that a knot would appear on the surface of the ball. This is what caused it to turn abruptly left. And he would have to take the ball out of play because of the damage inflicted. But what a shot! On this day the pros played from the same tees as the competitors and, with four holes to play, Tiger was two strokes ahead of John.

I distinctly remember John saying to all who would listen, "I cannot let a thirteen-year-old beat me." And he didn't. He birdied three of the last four holes to defeat Tiger by one stroke. Today, Tiger and John are very good friends. And I have seen them laugh and joke and tell others about that humid, torrid day in Texarkana.

CARING AND SHARING

Joy, Happiness, Giving Back, Fulfillment, Love

15

The importance of living life to the fullest can't be over-stated. Golf is a game about life. You learn; you experience; you share. The lessons one can absorb in a round of golf are often too precious to hoard. Life is not just about yourself. Life is about others. And one should share these feelings of life with others. Care for your fellow humans. Share your experiences, and contribute to the personal development of others.

Time is an accumulation of nows. There is no tomorrow; there is no yesterday; there is only now. It behooves all of us to live our lives one unique day at a time. Maximize the joy you have inherited as your birthright. Apply the lessons and the knowledge that you have gleaned from the wonderful game of golf. There is so much to be learned from this game—not just about yourself but about others.

In raising Tiger the consistent theme has always been that golf is a game—enjoy. Never have I imposed my likes, dislikes, desires, or attitudes on the development of this young man. Consequently, when he plays this beautiful game, the fundamental basis for his participation is the enjoyment of the process. In competition he never forgets what I taught him. It is a game—play it to the best of your ability, and enjoy yourself.

I don't seek to impose my personal beliefs or philosophies upon others. I only offer them for your examination, evaluation, and possible use. But when it comes to the rearing of children, I believe in sharing my insights and experiences.

SURPRISE! Tiger's mother, Tida, presents him to the people attending a surprise party at his home in honor of his first U.S. Amateur Championship.

Golf is growing by leaps and bounds worldwide. No longer is it the preserve of wealth and privilege. Now the less affluent are streaming onto the fairways in growing numbers.

Golf is a game for everyone. Enjoy it.

Mindful of golf's mushrooming popularity, the unimaginable good fortune this game has brought to him, and the need to reach out to others, Tiger has envisioned the establishment of a personal charitable foundation through which he can funnel some of the fruits of his labor to those in need. Initially, this foundation will address the problem of the self-image of our youth through the use of sports psychology techniques. Self-worth is a critical prerequisite for success. If Tiger can help to instill in countless other aspiring athletes the sense of pride and purpose that he has gleaned from his family and golf experiences, then he will have made a difference in the world that transcends tournaments and fame. For the true sweetness of victory lies not in simply savoring your own accomplishments but in passing the baton to give someone else the same opportunity. What my wife and I tried to do for Tiger, he now hopes to do for countless youths struggling to nurture a dream. Where will this lead him? We don't know. But that's another story.

INDEX